P9-EDF-423

AMERICAN SOCIETY FOR INDUSTRIAL SECURITY
1625 PRINCE STREET
ALEXANDRIA, VA 22314
(703) 519-6200

INTERNAL THEFT:
Investigation
&
Control

SE 28 '89

2659

LIBRARY
ASIS
1655 N.FORT MYER DR.
ARLINGTON, VA 22209

HV
6768
.I61
1975

INTERNAL THEFT:
Investigation
&
Control

An Anthology

Sheryl Leininger, Editor

Security World Publishing Co., Inc.
Los Angeles, Calif. 90034

Copyright © 1975 by Security World Publishing Co., Inc.

All rights reserved. No part of this book may be used or reproduced in any manner without written permission except in the case of brief quotations embodied in critical articles and reviews.

First Edition 1975
Second Printing 1976

Library of Congress Catalog Card Number: 75-17137

ISBN 0-913708-21-6

Security World Publishing Co., Inc.
2639 South La Cienega Boulevard
Los Angeles, California 90034

Printed in the United States of America

CONTENTS

III. EMBEZZLEMENT AND EXECUTIVE DISHONESTY

Section Two: INVESTIGATING INTERNAL THEFT

IV.   UNDERCOVER INVESTIGATION

Outline: Name and Aliases ° Necessary Papers ° Residences •
Criminal Records ° Membership in Organizations ° School Records
° Employment • Social Status • Physical Condition • Debts

VIII. INTERNAL THEFT CONTROLS

FOREWORD

Billions of dollars are lost each year to the employee thief. Today's businessman cannot afford to ignore employee dishonesty, for this growing problem, if left unchecked, can literally put him out of business.

Executives, managers, supervisors, security directors, as well as the student preparing for a career in loss prevention or business administration, will find in this volume a comprehensive look at internal theft through the eyes of experts. As an anthology, *Internal Theft: Investigation & Control* offers the reader a unique opportunity to study in one volume the experiences of more than twenty authorities directly concerned in one way or another with employee dishonesty. The contributors represent a wide range of occupations: security services, including investigation and polygraph. . .corporate loss prevention. . .accounting. . .insurance. . . interrogation. . .criminology. . .psychology. . .employee honesty and efficiency testing.

The book has been organized into three sections. The first defines the problem, exploring how and why employee theft occurs and who the problem employee is, from the warehouse pilferer to the computer embezzler to the dishonest executive. Section Two presents an overview of methods of investigating internal theft, including undercover investigation, interrogation and the use of the polygraph. The final section of the text is then devoted to the essential steps that can be taken to deter and control internal theft.

Sixteen of the chapters were published originally in *Security World* Magazine. The others, published here for the first time, are based on presentations from the International Security Conferences. Thanks are due to all of the contributors for their cooperation in reviewing and updating the material for this anthology.

Raymond C. Farber, President
Security World Publishing Co., Inc.

Section One:

THE PROBLEM
OF INTERNAL THEFT

I.
THE
THREAT
OF
EMPLOYEE
DISHONESTY

Chapter 1

CONFRONTING THE GROWING PROBLEM
OF EMPLOYEE THEFT

By Addison H. Verrill

Dun and Bradstreet reported that 13,061 companies went bank-rupt in 1966,[1] to the tune of $1.35 billion; and most of them went bankrupt in their first five years of operation. Losses due to employee theft contributed to many of these business failures.

One way to stop such theft, and stop it cold, is to give more and more authority to the security people within the company who can prevent theft—more power and status and more money for them-selves and their budgets. The security industry has come of age, and each year is a milestone. But with all our modern methods—our shopping surveys, inside operations, watchmen, guards, cameras, all sorts of electronic protection—employee dishonesty gets worse and worse.

Staggering Increase in Theft

It's not only the number of persons involved that's so stagger-

---

From a presentation given at the International Security Conference in New York City, 1968.
[1] In 1973, this figure was 9,345, according to Dun and Bradstreet.—Ed.

ing, it's the amount of the individual thefts. Formerly, the person who stole merchandise from a factory or warehouse would steal for himself or his friends. Today that man has graduated. . .he tries to steal enough so he can fence the stolen goods. He now steals to order. His fence needs three dozen size 15 shirts, and our employee thief has to get those shirts before the week is over. This kind of stealing isn't just old-fashioned pilfering. This is big business, and because of these thieves, security is becoming big business.

These are the cold, hard facts:

- During the past ten years there's been a 38% increase in employee dishonesty on the part of people who are handling cash. This fact was determined by taking statistics per thousand shopping tests for businesses throughout the country ten years ago against per thousand tests rendered today.
- Not only is there an increase in the number of people stealing, but the confessions of amounts stolen are larger by an even greater percent—45%—than they were ten years ago. In cash handling in the retail business, the average man or woman who in the past would take fifty cents from a transaction is now taking well over a dollar.
- As for employee theft of supplies in the merchandising industry, our statistics show a 43% increase within the comparable time of ten years. These results were obtained by figuring on a hundred inside operatives placed ten years ago against a hundred inside operatives placed today.
- The incidence of collusive theft among employees is higher than it has ever been. That means that today more and more thieves are getting their fellow workers to steal along with them. Consequently, when we do break cases today, we're finding more group involvement than before.
- It is not only the actual loss of money and merchandise that is causing profit statements to fall. The stealing of time is also a factor—time for which people are paid for really being on the job. Lack of accountability, violations of rules and procedures—these also cause loss.

A figure that is often mentioned for annual inventory shrinkage is $2 billion or $3 billion. It is probable that this doesn't come anywhere near the actual figure. There are several areas of employee dishonesty that are not counted when these statistics are compiled, such as top level employee theft—kickbacks, conflict of interest, embezzlement. There's even a problem of electronic embezzlement that we haven't yet figured into the yearly statistics. Computers are being used today instead of ordinary ledgers, and there are men who know how to beat the computers.

In one place a man was discovered to be transferring money from his company's bank account to his wife's account. He was feeding his own computer cards into the machine. This man would never have been caught if he hadn't broken down and admitted what he was doing. There were no books to examine; just a mass of magnetic computer tape. The feeling is growing that many big companies are being taken in this way who don't even know it yet, and no one knows the potential for dishonesty in this field.

Top Level Theft Adds to Totals

What about conflict of interest, kickbacks, and that kind of dishonesty? Should that aspect of dishonesty be figured in this total picture? If so, then that figure of $2 or $3 billion should be doubled. According to the U.S. Chamber of Commerce, this kind of manipulation alone is costing industry $3 billion a year.[2]

Most of this big-time stealing is hidden. In the past year or two there have been a couple of significant exposures on how and where it's being done. Consider the XYZ Company—a real manufacturing firm which had a scandal only a short time ago. The secretary of the executive vice president, the man in charge of marketing, owned the company which supplied XYZ with the cartons used for their products. This secretary's company was the exclusive supplier of these cartons, and her boss made all of the decisions for the company after she came to work for XYZ. She and the vice president had a profitable business going.

Another kickback story came out of another famous industrial firm. The traffic managers there were giving work only to those

---

[2] Chamber of Commerce of the United States, A HANDBOOK ON WHITE COLLAR CRIME (Washington, D.C., 1974), p. 6

stevedoring companies who were willing to pay them off. Retailing firms are notorious for kickback arrangements. At one of the largest not very long ago, investigators caught up with a coat-and-suit buyer who had taken kickbacks amounting to $500,000.

Since it's usually top executives who are involved in conflict of interest, in most companies the whole thing gets hushed up, and the worst that can happen to the offender is that he gets fired.

Leniency for Employee Thieves

This brings up an important point—that some segments in the business world are discriminated against in the manner of strict enforcement and the punishment of offenders. Let someone get caught stealing a thousand dollars from a bank, and invariably they go to jail. But let that same person be caught stealing a thousand dollars from business or industry, and the worst they wind up with is a suspended sentence.

This brings to mind the story about little Johnny who was caught stealing pencils from school. His father was called down and said, "I don't know why he should steal the pencils, because I bring him home enough boxes full from the office." For some reason our society is very timid in dealing with thieves in business and industry, perhaps because of the fact that we sometimes take home that box of pencils. Johnny's father is not demoralizing Johnny so much as he's demoralizing himself.

Methods of Fighting Theft

We're all being hurt by the continued spread of employee dishonesty. We're paying a higher price for everything we buy today in order for the businessman to absorb his losses from stealing. It's been said in many instances fully 5% of the price of an item is superimposed because of the very existence of the employee thief.

What should we do about this increasing problem of employee theft? Lately the question is being asked more publicly than ever. Full-page stories have appeared in national magazines illustrating the various ways in which an employee can steal from an employer. Is this kind of publicity the answer? Many think not. There is the risk that this could lead to the spread of the very sickness that it purports to criticize. It could teach more employees to steal. It could provide them with ideas and techniques they're better off not knowing.

How, then, do we hold back this rising tide of employee dishonesty? Let's look at it from the viewpoint of the shopping service or shopping test. If an organization is concerned about its inventory shrinkage problem and is using shoppers, whether from an outside agency or ones employed in-house, to test their employees, it should test for dishonesty only—disregard the reports for efficiency. When a shopper is burdened with long questions to be answered on the efficiency of an employee, it's going to detract from his ability at making an honesty test. There will be anywhere from 15% to 20% more results as far as employee dishonesty is concerned in retail shopping, if efficiency reports are dispensed with.

Important consideration should also be given to the part that inside operatives play in an operation today. After all, 80 to 85% of the inventory shrinkage of any magnitude involves merchandise and not cash. And that's the job to be handled by the inside operatives. Industry is using these undercover people in the wrong way when they hire an operative for four or five weeks only. Inside operatives should be hired for fifty-two weeks; they should be shifted from place to place; male and female operatives should be alternated. In this way, you're going to get the ultimate out of the undercover operative. And frankly, when an undercover operative is used on this basis, the confessions should come out to more money than was expended to pay for the operative.

The polygraph can also be an effective tool, not for mass testing, but for pre-employment screening and on specifics. It's essential to have a good, licensed polygraph examiner. An expert examiner must be a good interpreter of the charts and he must be a skilled interrogator.

In many instances, management does not make use of all the tools available to reduce their inventory shrinkage problem. They may call it a budget problem; more often the cause is timidity. This is a foolhardy and short-sighted policy. All too often, you'll hear about management expecting its security man to carry out an enormous task, to handle many multi-faceted problems. They expect to hire a security man for much less money than he's worth, and once hired, they resist giving him the tools and money that he needs to operate and do the job effectively. Then when there's an inventory shrinkage, who gets blamed? The security department.

This kind of thinking becomes less and less possible every year. A few years ago the man who represented security spoke more softly and hesitantly than he does today.

Ingenuity of Thieves

Let's move ahead of the thieves themselves so that we can think in terms of prevention and control, rather than in terms of blame and prosecution. One of the nation's largest mutual casualty insurance organizations reports that there are 407 basic ways of stealing from a business. Although it is not possible to list all the different ways that employees can steal, here are a few of the ingenious ways they can rob their bosses.

In a Buffalo foundry the employees stole 129,000 pounds of scrap lead out of the plant by making lead molds to fit around their bodies. In another company, the elevator operators in a large warehouse made a vault for themselves inside the elevator shaft. All they had to do was stop the elevator between the second and third floors, take out a few bricks from the wall and, lo and behold—there was a private warehouse.

Then there was the employee in a man's suit factory who stole a hundred thousand dollars worth of bolts of cloth without causing a shortage. How did he do it? This man was in charge of allocating the cloth for the suits. He would short the allocation by a quarter or an eighth of an inch per suit and build up enough of a backlog of material to take.

The trouble some thieves will go to is unbelievable. For a cigarette vending machine company, we uncovered the fact that the maintenance men in the office building at night were taking these heavy machines, lifting them up, turning them upside down and pocketing the money which came out of the chutes.

The explanations for dishonesty can sometimes be just as fantastic as the methods. One thief and embezzler was asked why he had stolen a hundred thousand dollars from his employer. He explained that he could tell that the business was failing; he merely wanted to put aside a nest egg, so that when business collapsed, his boss could make a new start.

In another example of this "ingenuity," the manager of a men's wear store, when he was warned of an impending inventory, borrowed enough merchandise from the friendly manager of a nearby branch to cover the stock depletion which he had been stealing. After the inventory was taken, he returned the merchandise to his pal in the other store.

Too often you will hear fantastic figures about inventory shortages—both too high and too low. But how was the inventory taken? How were the physicals taken? In the retailing firm, was there an accurate check on markups and markdowns? Was this done—was that done? And most of all, did the security department have anything to do with the physical taking of the inventory? The physical taking should be done with the assistance of security or at least partly under security control. Otherwise, the security department has to take the word of other executives who may not be as careful in the physical inventory taking. After all, the inventory shrinkage picture is at least a problem that the security department is going to have to live with. It's necessary, therefore, that they ascertain the correctness of any and all inventory figures.

Prevention Rather Than Detection

As previously noted, it is more important to strive for prevention than detection. How do we prevent these employees from stealing? Our experience suggests that incentive is more important than any other approach. Look for a moment at the normal figures for inventory shrinkages, from one-half percent to four or four-and-a-half percent in some instances. Frankly, there's at least one major retailing company that has much less than a 1% inventory shrinkage, and it's one of the largest in the country. That same company has an incentive plan—a profit-sharing plan, and a good one. Some of the employees, when they're ready to retire, end up with a profit-sharing bonus of anywhere from twenty to fifty thousand dollars.

Does that kind of incentive work? The shrinkage figures speak for themselves. The employee knows that even the smallest amount of stealing can result in the loss of all of his profit-sharing. And also, if he sees anybody else in the organization doing anything that will cause inventory shrinkage, he's quicker to report it to management because he has a vested interest. Give employees something to work for, give them a stake in the future of the company, and you'll have more people working on the side of management and on the side of security, instead of working against it.

There are too many people today being hired with no background check. We often find that employee thieves have been caught elsewhere or involved in something else.

There should be more regular meetings with employees where management and security people can teach them the problems that are involved that will create this inventory shrinkage. Speakers from outside the company who are experts in the field—the police department, court officials, outside organizations—these are all available to talk to employees of an organization with the idea in mind of assisting in this problem. A reward should be offered for reporting anything that might create an inventory shrinkage. The reward might be a dinner, or five dollars for finding anything that might go on.

In doing these things, it's important that employees are not made to feel that they are distrusted. If they feel this, the morale of personnel will be ruined. The behavioral scientists tell us that if an employee knows he is not trusted, he is liable to act in a negative and untrustworthy manner.

There should be greater efforts made in the sharing of information about employee thieves. There is, after all, communication among businessmen on bad checks, shoplifters, and certain other things. There's no clearing house for information about the employee thief who was caught stealing a thousand dollars in XYZ Company. There should be a focal point or a central organization for exchange of this type of information.

Businessmen should be more candid and honest when they're called for references on employees. All too often no answer is received to a request for a reference.

We should work together in our common cause. No one will entirely eliminate employee theft. That's an impossible dream. If we use all the resources at our command—and that includes the human resources, the honest and conscientious employee who wants to help—then we can at least control the situation.

Addison H. Verrill

Mr. Verrill is Board Chairman and Executive Vice President of Dale System Inc., a nationwide company over 43 years in the field of testing personnel honesty and efficiency. He joined the Dale System in 1933 and rose through the organization to assume its presidency and subsequently his present position.

A native of Connecticut, he has been an active member of the Chambers of Commerce for both Hamden and New Haven, Connecticut. He is a past chairman of the board of directors of the New Haven YMCA and a past president of the Hamden Lions Club.

Mr. Verrill has spoken widely on the subjects of business ethics, honesty and efficiency.

Chapter 2

EMPLOYEE THEFT:
WE CREATE OUR OWN PROBLEMS

By Leonard S. Lowell

·   The manager of one of the largest drive-in theaters in the East steals admissions from 100 cars a night by cleverly covering the automatic car counter with a false counter that looks the same, but does not record car movement.

·   The manager of a men's clothing store quietly finds out which of his employees are in debt and then recruits them into a theft ring to alter sales slips, arrange short shipments with vendors and mis-ring sales.

·   The parts foreman in an automobile assembly plant tapes small but highly expensive parts to his body every evening before he goes home.

Something in common among these thieves? Two things—beyond their dishonesty:

They are all confessed, identified, *prior thieves.*

And their new employers knew nothing about their past records.

© 1965, 1975 Security World Publishing Co., Inc.

These men were three of several thousand employee thieves recently surveyed by my organization who had prior "significant employee theft records." The study, which embraced 4,000 admitted thieves, revealed that fully 68 percent of them were repeaters in major thefts.

This is not surprising, of course. But what is astonishing is that slightly better than 98 percent of the employers of these men and women *did not know their past histories.*

Lack of Background Checks

We do not advocate that these people never get other jobs. But we do say their new employers are courting probable losses if they do not take the time—and, admittedly, the trouble—to find out just what is in the background of the people they consider for employment. And this is the core of the problem: employers, short-sighted in this area as many of us are in others, just do not bother to find out.

This neglect or irresponsibility is dynamite.

Anyone who steals does so, in part, because he thinks he can get away with it. He has successfully hidden the fact of his prior dishonesty (or dishonesties) from his current employer. He feels he can take a chance if the opportunity presents itself—or even if the opportunity requires a little searching out.

But suppose, for a moment, that his new employer tells him: "I know you have stolen before, but I think you have learned your lesson. I am willing to give you a fair chance. I assume you will be as fair to me."

In the light of this kind of candidness by an employer, the situation changes sharply. If the employee has any kind of conscience, he will appreciate the graciousness tendered him and respond in kind on the job. But even the employee who is inherently dishonest will realize that he is being accepted for what he is and that *he will be evaluated in the light of his past record.* If he steals again, he will not be considered and treated as a first offender who has "strayed into temptation."

Expensive Economy

But, regrettably, this kind of employer-employee conversation rarely occurs, because few employers know about prior records of the men and women they hire. Follow me through some recent, and very expensive illustrations:

•   The comptroller of a large women's wear chain was caught, after two years, using company funds to pay bills for a women's wear store operated by his brother. (His brother's store was competitive to one of the stores in the chain.) The comptroller had his brother's bills submitted to the chain and paid routinely with chain funds. If a supplier would not cooperate, the executive simply filled out a sticker, pasted it over his brother's firm name and then processed it within the chain. When interrogated with the aid of the polygraph, the comptroller admitted having paid the same brother's bills with money of his prior employer, a job he held for seven years and left, with commendation, to assume the comptrollership. Total damage to both employers: $75,000.

•   The manager of a wholesale auto supply house, who liked to live beyond his salary, kept two homes and three cars by operating his own wholesale business with his boss's merchandise on his boss's premises. He devised a system of internal thievery that included using company truck drivers to deliver goods to their private customers before servicing company customers and using company merchandise for a private mail order business operated in the basement of his home. An alert and honest young clerk finally realized his dishonesty and turned him in. Total damage: $39,000. Six weeks later, the deposed manager was hired as the manager of a brand-new and expensive supermarket in one of the nation's leading chains. Two weeks after that, he began to arrange with a vendor to make short shipments, sell the balance elsewhere and split the "profit" with him.

•   A food warehouse platform superintendent, apprehended for selling $3,000 worth of stolen foodstuffs and fired, was found to be doing the exact same thing for a food jobber in another city within three months. In both cases, he ripped labels off cans and bottles, turned them in for credits as damaged merchandise to keep inventory straight and sold the cans and bottles to institutions.

In all of these cases, the new employers knew nothing of the histories of these men. In all of the cases, only the most cursory pre-employment interviews were held and the most basic questions asked. No answers were checked, no recommendations examined.

Leniency Contributes to Loss

More than lax attitude by management is responsible for the ability of known employee thieves to get new jobs, where they are unknown, and steal again. A major share of the blame must go to two groups: law enforcement agencies who, with rare exceptions, believe that employee thieves are not important thieves; and employers themselves who refuse to prosecute when they are provided with evidence of employee chicanery.

By and large, employee thieves know that as long as they do not steal from a bank they are likely to get off without punishment from the courts. For some weird reason, dishonest bank employees steal "public" money as opposed to industrial thieves who steal "management" money.

For example:

• Officials of a major New England department store caught a woman sales clerk, a 16-year employee, in the act of pocketing receipts of a small sale. Under questioning, the woman admitted in writing to having stolen $18,000 from the store over the previous 15 years. The store pressed charges. At the hearing, the charges were revised to one of breaking the peace; the woman was fined $25 and even that was remitted. When store management, astonished at this treatment for a person who admitted having stolen $18,000, asked why she had been let off, they were told the confession was inadmissible. They were not told why.

• A clerk in a New York City department store, shortly after taking the job, stole a charge plate and used it 74 times within an eight-week period before being apprehended. He confessed in writing, yet received only a 30-day suspended sentence.

• Five employees of a Seattle liquor wholesaler were apprehended and confessed in writing to several thousand dollars in thefts. One man alone had taken more than $1,500. All received suspended sentences after defense counsel had pleaded for leniency, noting that each of the employees had lost his job and had therefore suffered enough.

Failure to Prosecute Is Factor

Management's reluctance to prosecute is the other side of the coin. The following are typical examples:

- A cashier in a midwestern discount center was caught selling merchandise at massive discounts to friends and sharing with them the "profits" from their later resale to friends and neighbors. He admitted having taken $13,000 in this manner over four years, yet management refused to press charges.
- A truck driver employed by a Southern plumbing supply house admitted having sold $45,000 of his employer's merchandise to the employer's regular customers over a long period of time for a fraction of the value. The store refused to prosecute.

Small wonder these people steal again. Why shouldn't they? They have little to lose.

The situation, in large part, comes down to the old maxim: "We often create our own problems; and we make our own solutions." Management creates a multifaceted problem for itself when it refuses to examine prospective employees and when it refuses to seek punishment for severe offenders so other members of industry will not be burned.

The place to catch potential troublemakers is in the employment office. The first and most important defense against crime losses is through screening of new employees. Dishonest men and women are dynamite once inside a business organization. The polygraph is perhaps the best answer to this question. We have found that it can disclose—in one hour—information about a prospective employee that may never be found with other means. Certainly the polygraph has demonstrated that it is far more accurate than a routine background investigation.

But however pre-employment screening is done, it must be done. Failure amounts to nothing less than incompetence on the part of the professional manager. He can have no complaint when an employee with a history for stealing steals again.

Leonard S. Lowell

When this article was written, Mr. Lowell was chief executive officer of Dale System, Inc., nationwide business-investigative and research organization. A co-founder of the company, he helped lead Dale from its first office in New Haven, Conn., to its current service of clients in every state of the country.

Mr. Lowell is currently a member of the board of directors and president of Hallmark Associates, Inc., a research subsidiary of Dale System. He resides in North Miami Beach, Florida.

Chapter 3

INTERNAL THEFT IN A RURAL COMMUNITY

Internal theft can happen anywhere. That is the message contained in the following interview, conducted by the editor of Hardware Retailing *and reprinted here by permission.*

The interview was tape recorded at the home of a Midwest hardware dealer. The name of the dealer has been changed to preserve his anonymity and prevent identification, but the story is told in his own words.

This account is not presented as a "model" case, nor does its appearance here constitute an endorsement of the procedures followed by the dealer. The story should, however, be of interest to anyone who has ever said, "It can't happen here."

Editor: Joe, I understand you had a problem of internal theft. Can you tell me what happened?

Joe: Well, I think maybe it would be well to tell you a little bit about the size of our town and our business. This is a rural community. We have 3,500 people in the town and we live in a county of

Reprinted with permission from HARDWARE RETAILING, published by the National Retail Hardware Association, Indianapolis, Indiana.

30,000. I am the third generation in the business—the store has been in operation 80 years, and we feel we are close to all our customers and employees.

Our employees are really more a part of the family and friends. We know their background, their families, their uncles and aunts; they grew up with us and around us. We've always had a great deal of trust in them. We've never considered any possibility of an internal theft problem.

We have 38 employees and the average tenure is 16-1/2 years. This includes little Distributive Education students who have been with us 6 months up to the people who have been with us for 40-some years.

There is no turnover; it isn't new, unfamiliar people who are working for us. We have had no suspicion of any internal theft and no reason to even think we had something to worry about.

About a month before last Christmas, I was snowed in at home. The phone rang. A man with a very gentle, compassionate voice said he was sorry to bother me but he had an important thing to discuss with me. He would not identify himself, but he told me that we had a problem with internal theft.

In talking with him, it seemed this wasn't the voice of someone trying to get even—there was compassion in the tone of his voice. He said that if necessary he would come forward voluntarily and help us solve the problem.

During the course of the phone conversation, he explained that we had three employees currently stealing from us: merchandise—not money. He then listed specifically about 30 or 40 items that he knew they had taken. Upon conclusion he reiterated that he would let me know who he was if he felt it was necessary, but he didn't want to get involved if he didn't have to.

The following day, Monday, I waited until about noon. Because my caller had told me that most of the theft occurred while I and my parents (who also are still active in the business) were at lunch, I called in three of our most trustworthy employees, ones whom I thought I could talk with, and related the Sunday afternoon conversation to them, named the three employees that were accused. . .

Editor: He had given you the names of the employees?

Joe: He had given me the specific names, one of which was my personal secretary, for whom I had the highest respect. She knew what I wanted almost before I asked for it and was the finest secretary that anybody could have. A young man who had recently been employed and a young girl who was a co-op student from the local school were the other two named.

Also, the caller had named one former employee that he knew had stolen from us and was still stealing, and another former employee who he thought had stolen, but he wasn't sure.

So, after acquainting the three trusted employees of our plight, my mother and father and I left for lunch. While we were at lunch, the first theft occurred. Our three people all witnessed it. The former employee came in, saw my secretary, told her that she wanted a scale to weigh herself. My secretary got up from her desk, got the scale, took it to the check-out counter, wrapped it, told the cashier that she'd charge it back at the office, and the former employee left with the scale. No charge came through.

The next day, another former employee, who had not been previously identified as a suspect, went through the same procedure with the same secretary. About three or four days later, the little Distributive Education student was seen to take an electric knife, wrap it at the counter, and tell the cashier that it would be charged through the office.

We let this go on for about a week. And at this point we contacted the local police, who called in the sheriff. We related to the police what had happened, and they suggested that we go another week and get more evidence. In that period we had the young man walk out with a hobby-horse, a toilet seat, five bathroom accessories, etc.

Editor: What did you do then?

Joe: After this two-week period, I confronted my secretary with the fact that we suspected she was stealing from us, and she immediately acknowledged that she was. I told her that I knew some of the things she had stolen, and I wanted her to list everything she had stolen. I implied that if she didn't, we would turn her over to the sheriff and see that she was sent to the state prison. She became quite emotional and broke down and started listing the merchandise she had taken, item by item, and dollar by dollar, over a two-year period.

When she had concluded her list she had named all the things on my list, plus approximately 100 other items—in fact, a total of almost $2,000 worth of merchandise. I then suggested that she list all of those people that she knew had stolen from us.

She did, and she named five other people, making a total of six people who had been stealing from us.

I then asked her to list for me all those people who had received merchandise from her or the others, knowing that it was stolen. She listed eleven other people in our community, making a total of seventeen.

Editor: What was your next step?

Joe: That same afternoon I approached the young student with the same procedure and the same development—she freely told me what she had taken, and she confirmed the others that were involved. All of this then led to a confrontation of all seventeen of them, with the sheriff in attendance and the police chief there, and our attorney. The total list of dollars in merchandise that had been taken and acknowledged came to $3,985. We don't know how much was taken that couldn't be remembered.

At this point it was suggested that we were willing to conclude the matter by having restitution in the amount of $4,000 by December 31, as a collective involvement. We wanted it made up one way or another from all those involved and would consider the matter closed if they did this.

It was a hard decision; we had a little conflict among ourselves. Two of us felt that we should prosecute, and two of us in the family felt that it should be resolved with as little problem as possible. On December 31 they brought the $4,000 in.

Editor: What was the argument used to convince you not to prosecute?

Joe: Well, the point was that too many families in the community were involved. These were all good, respectable people. They were not the kind of people you'd expect this to happen to. They were all brought up in a moral atmosphere. They were all respected by their fellow townspeople.

If we prosecuted them and sent them to jail, we would have caused a lot more trouble within their families, and within the personal involvements, than it was worth.

Editor: Did you get any indication of the thinking of the people who stole from you?

Joe: In talking with the people involved, the interesting thing is that they really didn't think they were stealing. They felt they were really entitled to it. It seemed to be an attitude of, "Well, we're working here and this is part of our compensation."

When we quizzed them about the possibility of taking money, in one instance we had the response: "Well, golly, I wouldn't *steal* from you! I wouldn't take money. But this is different, I just took some merchandise home and I didn't sell any of it; I just gave it away."

This is the interesting thing; I don't think in any case did anybody steal from us for financial gain, but rather simply to give a gift to their friend, or to their husband or wife. And those who accepted the merchandise knew that it was stolen, but didn't think of it as being a serious matter.

And that is pretty much the story of a little rural town where it is impossible to have somebody steal from you because you know them too well.

Editor: Has it become generally known throughout the community that this happened?

Joe: Well, one of the persons said, "Don't tell anybody!" The very next day, one of the mothers called me and said, "My daughter stole from you; don't tell anybody."

You can't keep something quiet when there are seventeen people involved.

Editor: Have you noticed any effect in the community, or have you encountered any conversation that would indicate that this has shaken the community?

Joe: No; in fact, I think many people are *amused* by it. They think it is a funny situation, not a moral thing; and this bothers me.

Editor: Have you taken any steps to advise other businessmen in your community that this happened?

Joe: The other business people are aware of it. We talked about it in our local Rotary club and discussed it with other organizations. We always get the same reaction: "We don't have this in our business; your business must be different."

I am inclined to believe that it occurs in every business around me and they just close their eyes to it.

Editor: Had you ever had any previous warning about something like this?

Joe: About two weeks before I had my anonymous phone call, I had a general business letter from our supplier, suggesting that internal theft was of serious consequence in our industry.

At the time I showed my father the letter, I remarked, "Thank God we don't have this problem in our store. I am glad I am not in the metropolitan area where it might occur. We know our people. It can't happen to us."

At the time I threw the letter in the waste basket. Since then I have obtained copies of the letter, and sent them to all my business acquaintances with a postscript, "It *can* happen to you."

Editor: Did you have any problem with any of the accused threatening action against you for anything that you said or did?

Joe: Three of the people who were accused by our employees of having received merchandise threatened to sue us for defamation of character, etc., and made quite a point of their position that they had not stolen anything and were absolutely innocent, and that we were in trouble for accusing them.

We had been very careful, however, to have the employees who were stealing from us do the accusing; we never accused anyone. The girls wrote the names down in their own handwriting, and the accusations were witnessed. At the point of calling the sheriff and the police chief, we only gave the evidence that the girls had given us, so that we were completely free of accusing anyone.

When this was brought to the attention of the three, their attorneys immediately stopped any action and suggested that they settle. In all three cases they then admitted that they had received the merchandise knowing that it was stolen and threw themselves on the mercy of our judgment.

Editor: Have you learned how this began?

Joe: I asked one girl why she had stolen from us. She said that she really didn't know; it was just something that developed.

This girl is very highly thought of in the community. She has a lovely family; she is married to a fine man. She had grown up here for a generation—part of the town, not some stranger here.

I said to her, "Why? Tell me why you stole."

She said, "I don't know, but I can tell you the first thing I did take. One night as I was leaving, I was in a hurry, it was late, and I remembered as I was going out the back door that my husband wanted a starter for the fluorescent light fixture in his workshop. I came back to the counter and picked up this starter, and thought to myself, 'Well, I'll pay for it tomorrow,' and I didn't.

"That's the first thing I stole."

This was simply such an easy thing to do that it progressed from there, from a 29¢ starter for a fluorescent light, on to approximately $4,000 worth of merchandise.

II.
WHY
EMPLOYEES
STEAL

Chapter 4

MOTIVATING FACTORS IN
EMPLOYEE THEFT

By Wallace Rash

What are the motivating factors that cause certain people to steal?

First of all, there is the kleptomaniac—the person with an irresistible, neurotic urge to steal. Although rare, this is one of the motivating factors that could make an employee steal from his employer. If our security problems depended on the kleptomaniac, many of us would not have any work to do. These people actually cause very little loss to business.

Another factor is the impulse to steal. This might be a one-time situation where an employee had the opportunity, the desire, the nerve and the thought that he could possibly get by with this theft, and he would take a chance to steal something on impulse. This particular type of theft, of course, is not planned or rehearsed. This also occurs to some degree in outright shoplifting by customers in a store.

A third motivating factor is the employee's monetary need or desire for monetary gain from the theft of goods, merchandise, or

From a presentation given at the International Security Conference in Los Angeles, 1967.

money from his employer. Usually there are many secondary motivating factors that create this situation. The fact that the person is not making enough money to get along on is in most cases only a symptom of his problem. Usually the person who cannot get by on his salary has expensive habits. His outgo exceeds his income.

Actual monetary need is one of the less frequent reasons for employee theft. Of course, there are some cases where pressing medical expenses, a change in pay scale, or loss of overtime work may put a financial strain on an employee. But only on rare occasions will a person admit to having stolen from his employer strictly because he needed the money.

Another motivation for theft is "social need." The social need is especially prevalent where many young people are employed. One of them will steal something and then the others will do it to keep even.

For example, retail grocery chains sometimes hire 15 or 20 students to work part-time after school. Almost always you'll find these young people will eat two or three apples, a banana, a package of cookies or two—and some of them can eat $8 or $10 worth of groceries during an afternoon's work. They don't realize how much that apple really cost, and how much that grocery store has to sell in order to make up the cost. This is the accepted thing in their social group.

Often insecurity on a job tends to create a motivation to steal. When the relationship between the employee and the employer is not ideal, the employee has no feeling of loyalty towards his employer. Perhaps the employer provides no benefits for him, nothing to add to his incentive to be an honest, trustworthy employee. Consequently, if the opportunity presents itself, he may steal.

A man might begin to steal because of marital problems. He may be having problems at home and want to get some sympathy from his wife. We've had several occasions where an employee steals something and then goes home and tells his wife about it, hoping that she will be sympathetic and hoping to patch up the difficulties they were having.

Opportunity Is Tempting

A major factor in employee theft is lack of proper security measures. When there are no proper security measures, employees have an ever-present opportunity to steal. There are no strict policies against theft; there is no discipline for the offenders who are caught stealing. Management may discharge them, try to make a little recovery if they can, and that's the end of it. The people know that if they are caught, the worst they can do is lose the job—and maybe it's not a very good job anyway.

The opportunity to steal is the one thing that we, as security people, can help prevent.

Even checking the background of a prospective employee is not a guarantee that he will not succumb to temptation. My firm once tested and interviewed a young man as a prospective employee for a chain of convenience stores. We found nothing derogatory in his application or interview. We gave the prospective employer a favorable report, and the young man was hired.

About two months later we received a call from a supervisor of the chain. He said, "Are you sure you haven't made some mistake in recommending this fellow for employment? We put him to work in one of the stores, and on his fourth day we caught him stealing some cigarettes. We talked to him about it, but three days later, we caught him stealing again. Are you sure you had no report that he had ever stolen from a previous employer?"

A check through his file revealed that he had been working in a gravel pit all his life—there was nothing to steal there. When he finally got the opportunity to steal, he couldn't withstand the temptation.

One motivating factor that may be hard to accept is the fact that the employer may be dishonest himself. As a result, the employee does not feel he has to be honest.

For example, one company in our area would hire common labor at the minimum wage and tell them they would receive a raise after three months. Generally the people would not stay three months in the first place. But if they did, they would ask for their raise but would not receive it. This was a dishonest act on the part of the employer. He had no intention of giving a raise—he only wanted to give the employees some incentive to work at least the three months. In this sort of relationship between the employee and the employer, the obligation to be honest and try to do the right thing is destroyed.

Sometimes a clerk in a drugstore or grocery store is instructed by his employer to overcharge a penny here and there to make up for shortages. When an employee is instructed to steal from the customers, his loyalty to the company is destroyed and he has no guilt feeling about stealing a few bucks from the employer.

Rationalizations for Theft

One of the greatest reasons for employee dishonesty is rationalization on the part of the employee, because of real or imagined unfair treatment by the employer. If the employee feels he's been treated unfairly, he can rationalize in his mind. . . "Well, I worked ten hours overtime last month and didn't get paid for it, so I didn't see anything wrong with taking a couple of bucks, or getting a few gallons of gas out of the company gas pump."

Physical or verbal abuse on the part of the employer certainly would contribute to this unfair treatment motivation, as would lack of incentives for honesty. If an employee is caught stealing and is asked why he started to steal, he'll think of 14 different reasons why he feels justified in stealing because of something his employer has done.

Another motivating factor might be called the "monkey see, monkey do" effect. If a rank-and-file employee sees other people, especially those in supervisory capacity, stealing or doing anything that would be costly to the company, he sees no reason not to do the same. A group of high school boys drinking a few sodas in a store is one thing; a group of higher management people showing no regard for security or honesty is something more serious. This gives employees an automatic excuse for doing wrong. "Well, old so-and-so, the supervisor, did it, why shouldn't I? If it's all right with him, it's okay with me."

Employee theft sometimes exceeds the "monkey see, monkey do" stage. In interviewing former employees of large aircraft plants in our area, we have found that almost always they would admit a few small thefts. When asked if they had ever stolen anything from a place where they worked, their standard answer would be, "Well, a few nuts, screws and bolts. . .maybe a few drill bits."

One subject's polygraph test indicated that there was something more serious than just "a few nuts and bolts." He finally admitted that in his garage he had three nail kegs. Every day when he got home from work, he would put the nuts in one keg, the screws in another and the bolts in another. When the three kegs were full, he would sell them to a junk yard. This man was stealing because he knew he could get by with it. He could carry these things out in his pockets without being searched.

The final factor is the employee who has total disregard for the accepted standards that have been set. This particular person is hard to cope with. He doesn't have any regard for anyone's personal property or the law itself. He would not hesitate to steal anything of any value if he thought he had a possible chance to get away with it.

We have heard about the "moral decay" of the working public. With more people working today, there are more people who have less regard for accepted standards. This has contributed, unquestionably, to the two billion dollars that has been stolen in a year. There's nothing that we as security people can do about the moral decay of the present generation. The thing that we *can* do is to increase our security precautions. If we can reduce temptation by convincing management that security is everyone's business, by installing a security program that makes all employees security-conscious, then we will have—perhaps—helped reduce this two billion dollar loss.

Wallace R. Rash

Mr. Rash is presently vice president of Cannon Protective Services, Inc., a multi-service security firm in Houston, Texas.

After serving with the U.S. Air Force during World War II, Mr. Rash spent ten years with the Dallas Police Department, including seven years as a detective in the Burglary and Theft Division. In 1956 he entered private security as a polygraph examiner.

During 16 years with Smith Protective Services, Inc., Mr. Rash advanced from the position of staff examiner to become president and general manager. The company's services included polygraph, industrial investigations, guard and courier service, and fire protection.

A graduate of the Keeler Polygraph Institute, Mr. Rash is a charter member of the American Polygraph Association and a board member of the Texas Association of Polygraph Examiners.

Chapter 5

A BEHAVIORAL PSYCHOLOGIST
LOOKS AT THEFT

By Dr. Howard Newburger

Thievery has become one of the largest industries in our country. It gainfully employs more people than almost any other activity or industry on either side of the fence of legality. Who steals, and why? I will outline here five major types of people who become involved in theft, as well as some of the strategies that might be developed in order to minimize participation in theft.

Social Change as a Factor

This first category of theft motivation is somewhat theoretical. We're dealing here with forces that we really cannot see or feel immediately, although they do show up at the bottom of the ledger at the end of the year when industries and corporations are concerned with losses due to thievery. But the causes of this particular source of crime are somewhat obscure. Because we are in the middle of it, it is difficult for us to see the fact that we're undergoing an enormous social change. Marriage and family patterns, for

From a presentation given at the International Security Conference in Washington, D.C., 1972.

example, are changing. For every 100 marriages that take place in a period of time, there will be 50 divorces.

People are becoming more self-sufficient today. They have more leisure time in which to do more things. Previously disadvantaged groups are coming increasingly into their own. As a result of these changes, people are becoming looser; old ways are breaking down.

We have people today without inner structure, without inner controls, because they've learned that the old ways of living are somewhat archaic and antiquated. At the same time, we have very sophisticated advertising campaigns based on conspicuous consumption. People are under all sorts of pressure to buy things. There is increased mobility; people can travel around more and see things they don't have. Lacking inner controls and yearning to acquire material possessions, people may succumb to the temptation to steal.

We conducted a small experiment when I was vice president of a petroleum exploration company. We had quite a bit of theft of drill bits and other equipment. We tried to make the atmosphere more military in character, less casual and easy-going. We laid down strict rules; we emphasized the importance of being at work on time, putting in a full day's work. The men in supervisory positions were ordered to present a picture of very tight control. The workers were to be told—although courteously—exactly what they would be doing. In a sense, we were giving the men an external structure.

Under these circumstances, theft was greatly reduced. There is no way of knowing for sure, of course, whether the reduction was a direct result of this tightening control, or was due to other factors.

It is logical to conclude, however, that it is virtually impossible to keep a company in the black when the workers are rather casually dealt with and are not afforded tight supervision and control.

Psychopathic Personalities

To my knowledge, there is no effective way of preventing the psychopathic thief from stealing. Most repetitive thieves come from the psychopathic ranks. A psychopath is an individual, generally above average in intelligence, who has no fear of consequences. He is not concerned with the outcome of his actions. He cannot make long-range plans. He does not think in terms of "If I do this, such-and-such will happen." He has no conscience. Usually a conscience is something that we all develop in our childhood. If we have a fairly good relationship with our parents, we take on their values and ideas about what is right and wrong. The psychopath, however, does not assume these values.

Sometimes security directors may be fooled when they apprehend a psychopath. Some psychopathic thieves will appear quite remorseful if caught. . .they may cry, plead, bring up soul-wrenching arguments about why they should be dealt with leniently. But—and this is the acid test which separates the psychopathic from the non-psychopathic individual—their anxiety is not because they've done something wrong, but because they've been caught.

So far, correctional methods have not been effective in changing the psychopathic personality. Incarceration will not stop him from stealing; once released, he will go right back and steal again. He does not think of the consequences of his actions. We have no means of keeping the psychopath from stealing—other than having a highly visible security force. In the absence of an internal conscience, we have to be concerned with creating an external conscience. A large, highly visible security force and complete electronic protective devices are the best deterrents I know of for the psychopath. He will not change; but he will not come to the well-protected business or store. He will go elsewhere to continue his theft career.

Group Expectations

In certain sections of our cities there are subcultures where adolescents do not meet the expectations of their group unless they have been involved in crime. Part of the social norm is to steal, be sent away to a reformatory, come out, and later be sent back again. People who grow up in these areas are brought up to be expected to steal. They steal for two reasons: to demonstrate bravery, like the Indian tribes who considered it a great *coup*, or honor, if they could get into the teepee of an enemy while he slept and take something of his; or for profit—a source of income.

The best defense for this type of theft is to develop an image and let it be known publicly that certain people who were caught stealing from a particular facility are being dealt with very harshly. Newspaper stories or other media could publicize a severe sentence imposed on an apprehended thief. Invariably this sort of publicity will result in reduced thievery from that particular plant facility or installation. . .just as in the state of Delaware, where flogging is permitted as punishment, theft statistics are low. The foot-loose, fancy-free thief working his way across the country will bypass Delaware.

You cannot flog employees literally, of course. . .but you can flog them symbolically. You can make it a public relations job to let it be known publicly how harshly offenders are dealt with.

Irrational Motives in Thievery

Some people will steal things not because they need the money or the merchandise; not because their subculture suggests that they commit theft; but because of some irrational, unconscious, obscure motive. Some people steal in such a way that they know they are going to be caught. This is unusual; most thefts are never solved. Anyone with reasonable intelligence could probably steal and get away with it. People with irrational motives, however, may actually want to get caught.

One fellow, for example, stole some sports jackets from a department store. He would have gotten away with it, except for the fact that he later brought the jackets back to the store's dry cleaning division to be cleaned. He was obviously out to get himself caught. We can often tell what people's real motivations are by observing the outcome, the net result, of their actions. The net result of this fellow's actions was to be sent away to prison. He was happy to "pay his debt to society."

Often people feel uneasy or tense because they feel they have done something wrong. Every time there is a major crime committed, hundreds of people will confess to it. They may have been miles away from the scene of the crime and could not possibly have had anything to do with it. Yet they confess. They want to be punished in some way for their deep guilt feelings.

In the category of thefts induced by irrational or unconscious causations, there are people who are primarily motivated by a desire to be caught. The very act of being caught and possibly incarcerated will provide sufficient punishment to expiate or satisfy their guilt feelings. If people feel they have done something wrong, have sinned in some way—and sins can be of thought as well as of deed—they are going to square things for themselves in some way. Sometimes it may mean having an automobile accident, or becoming accident-prone. Or it may mean committing an illegal act toward the end of getting the embarrassment, punishment, humiliation associated with apprehension.

The irrationally motivated thieves are people whom you would not expect to steal. There is no readily apparent reason for their crimes. If you talk to them or, rather, listen to them for a while, however, you will begin to recognize their guilt feelings. They are out to get expiation for their sins.

The strategy for dealing with these people is not to give them what they are after, but rather to shock them with something totally unexpected. To someone who is expecting severe punishment, this could be a surprising statement such as, "Oh, thank you for picking up that expensive handbag. We were going to move it into another department anyway. So long." Or if someone expects a slight slap on the wrist, the shock would be in treating him severely. The problem here, of course, is the very short period of time available to assess these types. This takes training and reading.

Industrial Sabotage and Absenteeism

This fifth category is very widespread. Sabotage and absenteeism are really subtle forms of thievery that cause loss to business and industry.

An example of sabotage is the employee who threw a soft drink bottle into the tire mold at a tire plant. He did not care about the work he was doing; he had no pride in it. He saw the president of the company drive in each day in his beautiful, expensive new car, while he himself drove an old compact car that needed a motor job.

Absenteeism is a form of stealing by not giving full value for pay received, by exploiting liberal sick-time allowances. Absenteeism costs millions of dollars each year. In a Boston department store, a study was done on the people who were absent during the year from illness. About 72% of them had not really been physically ill. They had no real desire to work and to give value for their pay.

There are a couple of solutions to these problems. This type of sabotage and absenteeism takes place only under certain conditions. Impersonalization in terms of the treatment of the employee is a major contributing factor. Employees may be designated by numbers; management may be remote, aloof from the workers. The employee treated in an impersonal manner is going to look for possible ways to get even.

People want to feel important. They may even take their lives or become insane if they do not have a feeling of significance. If we are able to develop ways of making people feel important and significant, the problems of sabotage and absenteeism will be reduced.

Andrew Carnegie, the steel magnate, would go down on the floor among the steel workers every day, with his sleeves rolled up so he looked like one of them, shaking hands and talking to the men. He was successful in preventing his workers from feeling impersonalized.

The Hawthorne experiments indicated the importance of workers being made to feel they are not taken for granted. In this experiment, the company was interested in improving production. They instituted a morning coffee break, and found that production went up following the break. They established an afternoon coffee break, and production again rose. Men were working less and producing more. They put in music, and production increased. They installed a special counseling service for the employees. Production rose. Then they took away all the new benefits, and production still continued to rise. Why? The workers were made to feel they were part of something; something was being done to them.

Clearly, one way to cut into the statistics of theft and loss as a result of sabotage and absenteeism is to personalize the relationships with the workers. The security force can be very helpful here in terms of getting to know the names of the workers, mixing with them. The security force is the visible enforcement arm of management. They can help to make the employees feel important.

Howard M. Newburger

In addition to his private practice as a psychologist, Dr. Newburger is currently a psychological consultant for the Harrison, N.Y., Police Department. He also serves as Chairman of Faculty and Supervisor of Psychotherapy at the Institutes of Applied Human Dynamics.

Formerly Dr. Newburger was Chief Psychologist at the New Jersey State Correctional Facility at Annandale; lecturer and conductor of psychoanalytic training at the United Nations (Division of Social Defense); an associate professor at New York Uni-

versity; Psychology Coordinator, Prelect, John Jay College of Criminal Justice (a major program for the training of the New York City Police Department).

He is the co-author of Winners and Losers *(with Marjorie Lee), published in 1974.*

III.
EMBEZZLEMENT
AND
EXECUTIVE
DISHONESTY

Chapter 6

EMBEZZLEMENT: ROBBERY BY TRUST

By Dr. Donald R. Cressey

Three major explanations of embezzlement are found in the published material on the subject. According to the first kind of explanation, embezzlements are the products of a variety of factors, any one of which or any combination of which may produce the crime. In the second explanation, the cause of embezzlement is said to lie in poor systems of accounting and lack of detailed checks on persons in positions of trust. A variation of this explanation is that embezzlement results from "desire" and "opportunity." According to the third explanation, the cause of embezzlement lies in the constitutional or mental make-up of the embezzler.

In my attempt to explain the behavior of embezzlers it was necessary to take into account the data reported to support these various theories. I proceeded by trying to formulate a generalization that applied to all of my cases, and to all other data available. After four unsuccessful attempts, what I came up with—to put it briefly—was the idea that embezzlement involves three essential kinds of psychological processes:

Trusted persons become trust violators when they (a) conceive

©1965, 1975, Security World Publishing Co., Inc.

of themselves as having a financial problem which is nonshareable; (b) have the knowledge or awareness that this problem can be secretly resolved by violation of the position of financial trust; and (c) are able to apply to their own conduct in that situation a verbalization which adjusts their conceptions of themselves as trusted persons with the conception of themselves as users of the entrusted funds or property.

The first of these ideas, the idea of the nonshareable problem, has been given the most attention by observers, reviewers, and critics, but I think it is probably less important than the second and third ideas. All that is necessary for an unshareable problem is to have a financial situation that is of such a nature that the ordinary sources of money for solving it are unavailable. For example, a businessman who loses his fortune in the stock market may be unable to confess this fact to his wife, friends, and associates; he then has a nonshareable problem. When they look back at the situation, embezzlers almost invariably say that they were "foolish," "had too much false pride," or make some similar statement, but at the. moment the fact is that *from their perspective* they simply are unable to borrow the money or get it from their ordinary sources. I found an example in a recent "Advice to the Lovelorn" column:

> Dear Ann: "I fear I may need psychiatric help. I'm a bookkeeper in a small firm. I needed some money to pay bills which have been long overdue and on my mind. I took $75 out of the petty cash fund and marked the slip 'balanced.'
>
> "I could have gone to my boss and received a loan for this amount with no trouble, but I had too much pride. My husband makes a small salary, and I was ashamed to admit we were having financial problems.
>
> "I'm paying the money back at the rate of $15 a week. In three weeks I'll have it all paid back, and no one will know it was missing. But I have a horrible fear that one day I'll take a much larger amount and be unable to replace it. Then I'll be in serious trouble.
>
> "Don't suggest a clergyman; I've never been a churchgoer. Should I see a psychiatrist?"
> ——Ashamed

After I had formulated the non-shareable-problem notion, I tested it by asking about fifty embezzlers their opinions about a financial problem or "emergency" which would be a shareable one. This was a crude test, to be sure, but it did work out. I asked them to suppose that for some reason their fire insurance policy had lapsed and then, through no fault of their own, there was a short in the wiring or lightning struck and their home burned down. I asked them then to assume that they lost everything that they owned. All they had left in the world was the clothing on their own and their family members' backs. My question then was, "Do you think that in a situation like that one you would have been tempted to do what you did?" Sixty percent of the cases indicated quite clearly that the nonshareable element is absent in the hypothetical situation and that they therefore would not embezzle in it. The remainder avoided the situation. Here are four responses to my question:

"No. I don't believe I would take it. I think that in a case like that folks would have sympathized with me and helped me out. There would be outside aid."

"No. I'd just work it out. My wife would know about it and we could work it out together."

"No. There you take a different attitude. You can buy on credit, and you'd be so wrought up about the disaster and so enthusiastic about the new purchases that the relationship would not be parallel."

"Well, I don't doubt that I would if I couldn't borrow the money or something of the sort. There are people or relatives that have money. I've never got along with them, but if it was a necessity like that I would go to them."

Embezzler's Self Image

Embezzlers must be able to justify a trust violation to themselves without regarding themselves as criminals. The person must also see an opportunity to solve his problem in secret by violating the trust which has been placed in him. This opportunity is actually highly relevant, but it is connected with the first and third processes in such a way that we need give it no emphasis here. The theoretical problem here is a problem in psychological perception of the opportunity to embezzle. Let me give you one

statement, made by an accountant (embezzler), about the opportunity to embezzle and the techniques of embezzlement:

> "In my case, I would have to say that I learned all of it
> in school and in my ordinary accounting experience. In
> school they teach you in your advanced years how to
> detect embezzlements, and you sort of absorb it. . .it is
> just like a doctor performing abortions. In his medical
> training he must learn to conduct the abortion, because
> many abortions are necessary for the health of the mother.
> Maybe he will perform a few legitimate abortions, and
> then an illegitimate one. He has learned to conduct the
> illegitimate one in his ordinary medical training, but he
> would have to include all of his courses in physiology,
> anatomy, and everything else, as well as the specific
> technique. In my case I did not use any techniques
> which any ordinary accountant in my position could
> not have used; they are known by all accountants, just
> like the abortion technique is known by all doctors."

I am convinced that the third process mentioned in the generalization, the process of verbalization, is the crux of the individual
embezzlement problem. This means that the *words* that the
potential embezzler uses in his conversation with himself actually
are the most important elements in the process which gets him into
trouble, or keeps him out of trouble. First of all, remember that
he is in a position of trust. Because he is in a position of trust he
necessarily has general and sometimes technical information about
trust violation.

When one learns the concept of honesty, he learns the concept
of dishonesty; when he learns to prevent defalcations, he learns how
to perpetrate defalcations, and so on. Now he defines a financial
problem as a nonshareable one which then, by definition, must be
solved by an independent, secret, and relatively safe means if it is
going to be solved at all. Next he identifies the possibilities for
resolving the problem by violating the trust, and if he sees a
possibility, it is because he defines the relationship between the
nonshareable problem and an illegal solution to that problem
(embezzlement) *in language which enables him to look upon trust
violation as something other than trust violation.* Most commonly

the embezzler at this point uses language which enables him to look upon trust violation as essentially noncriminal. If he does not do so, he does not become an embezzler.

To illustrate, suppose we have a man who is a pillar of the community, a respected honest employee. This man finds himself with a nonshareable problem, and an objective opportunity to solve the problem by stealing from his company. The chances are very good that if in that situation I walked up to the man and said, "Jack, steal the money from your boss," he would look at me in horror. However, honest and trusted men do "borrow," and if he tells himself that he is borrowing the money he can continue to believe that he is an honest citizen, even as he steals the boss blind.

But I do not wish to overemphasize the idea of "borrowing," for there are many verbalizations used, some of them quite complex. I use it as an example of a vocabulary that will adjust for contradictory roles: the role of an honest man and the role of a crook.

It should be emphasized that vocabularies of motive are not something invented by embezzlers (or anyone else) on the spur of the moment. There are many illustrations of ideologies, popular in our culture, that sanction crime: "Honesty is the best policy, but business is business." "It is all right to steal a loaf of bread when you are starving." "All people steal when they get in a tight spot." "Some of our most respected citizens got their start in life by using other people's money temporarily."

These are personalized into: "My intent is only to use the money temporarily so I am borrowing, not stealing." "I have been trying to live an honest life but I've had nothing but troubles, so to hell with it."

Embezzlement on the Rise

I believe that the embezzlement rates in the United States have been increasing in recent years, and I think it can be safely predicted that they will continue to increase unless a significant preventive program is introduced. During the next ten years, the professional work group and the clerical work group certainly will continue to grow in numbers and inportance. Business organizations are increasing in size and complexity, technology is being advanced at an accelerated rate and is being applied at an accelerated rate, leaving a higher percentage of the labor force in the white collar class. It is in this white collar class where we find all our "trusted employees," and accordingly it is this white collar class that embezzles our money. Census statistics are not classified in a way that gives much help here, but census data do indicate that workers classed as "professional," "technical," "managers," "officials," "proprietors," and "clerical workers" rose from 30% of the labor force (in 1940) to 43% (in 1963).

We do not know much about the attitudes of clerks, nor for that matter do we know much about the managers, officials, and proprietors. But a number of studies have been made of "professional" and "technical" workers, probably because they have become so important in business. What we know about the professional workers is that, by and large, they are unhappy. One survey of 587 professional employees conducted by the University of Chicago's Industrial Relations Center concluded that the professionals are definitely less satisfied than skilled workers, foremen, salesmen, and management. "In practically every group which has been surveyed, with the exception of a relatively few places, there was strong evidence of frustration and general dissatisfaction." In a similar study of 622 engineers and scientists, 18 percent felt that they were underpaid compared with other groups and 76 percent thought that management tried to manipulate people for their own purposes.

We have then a continuation of the trend in the character of business transactions that made it necessary to trust employees. Now the percentage of the labor force in the category where we find trusted persons is going up. Moreover, business procedures are becoming so complex that the whole fabric of an enterprise depends more and more upon men who have been given independent control over some segment of the enterprise. If nothing else changes, we should expect the embezzlement rates to continue to go up. Can we stop it from doing so by changing the white-collar workers' conditions of employment?

If my generalization has any validity, then a potential embezzlement can be blocked at either the nonshareable problem point or the verbalization point.

Trust violation rates might be reduced rather drastically by means of company programs designed to eliminate the number of nonshareable problems among employees. Since most of the nonshareable problems are financial, this means development of programs that are of such a nature that employees (a) have few financial problems, or (b) have financial problems that can be shared, preferably with the employer. In his book,[3] Norman Jaspan reports that his management consulting firm found dishonesty in 50 percent of the assignments it undertook in one year, when there was no prior hint of dishonesty. That is, his firm makes surveys of employee morale, performance, in connection with plant layout, efficiency, and other matters which are essentially *engineering* in nature. *In these cases* they found dishonesty in 50 percent. He does not give the total number of cases that the company investigated during the year, but he does indicate that in 1959 his staff unearthed $60,000,000 worth of dishonesty with more than 60 percent attributable to supervisory and executive personnel.

Jaspan makes a recommendation regarding prevention which is consistent with the notion that the incidence of nonshareable problems can be reduced. He recommends that businessmen know the status of employee morale, saying that "nothing creates shortages so rapidly and so surely, or reacts quite so adversely on customer good will, as resentful and disgruntled personnel. Whenever a low morale exists, the invariable result is theft on the one hand and bad customer relations on the other."

Jaspan then tells of one company which has a program called "Tell it to Tom." Tom is an employee with long service who has the confidence of his fellow workers and of management as well. Tom's job is to listen to his co-workers' complaints and personal problems, whether they concern the company or their private lives. He brings the employee's gripes to the attention of management and can marshal the firm's forces in helping an employee who is having personal difficulty. He also will call on public and private agencies if that is necessary.

Employee Education

Educational programs emphasizing the nature of the verbalization commonly used by trust violators could be introduced for employees. It seems to me that such an approach would enable a

---

[3]Norman Jaspan, THE THIEF IN THE WHITE COLLAR. (Philadelphia: J.B. Lippincott Co., 1959).

larger portion of trusted persons to realize that *they* could become trust violators and to identify with nonviolators when nonshareable problems occur. I am proposing that we make it increasingly difficult for trusted employees to, for example, think of themselves as "borrowers" rather than as "thieves" when they take the boss's money. It is highly probable that our current practices in this regard actually encourage embezzlement. That is, we tend to emphasize the same notion that the bonding companies and others emphasize, namely that embezzlement occurs among people who are the victims of "wine, women, and wagering." Because this lore is so popular, a person with a nonshareable problem who is not gambling, drinking, and running around with women can easily think of himself as a nonembezzler who is simply "borrowing." On the other hand, one who has accepted a position of trust in good faith, which after all is necessary in order that he get into the population of persons who can be potential violators of trust, and who has become firmly convinced that he would be a "crook" or "thief" or "embezzler" if he "borrowed" would find it as difficult to "borrow" as to "rob" or "steal." One rationalization for the crime of embezzlement, "borrowing," would not be available.

This is a quite simple idea, but its implementation might be very difficult. Whether we are thinking about embezzlement or any other type of crime, our conception of ourselves as potential criminals depends upon our general characterization of criminals. To a large extent, we think about criminals in terms of "ideal types." For example, when I say the word "criminal" you are likely to picture a square-jawed, bewhiskered tough wearing a striped sweat shirt. Since you are neither square-jawed, bewhiskered, nor stripe shirted, you do not see yourself in the picture. The fact is, of course, that criminals do not look any different from anyone else, and it is partly for this reason that prisoners have said to me, "But I am not really a criminal." Just as you think the criminal does not look like you, they think the criminal is someone that did something they did not do. They will admit that they perpetrated the offense for which they have been convicted, but they think the *real* criminal is the man down the cell block, the one who perpetrated an offense quite different from the one perpetrated by the observer. Thus, the child molester thinks of the robber as the *real* crook, but the robber says, "Well, at least I didn't swindle any widows or orphans like the confidence man."

The confidence man, in turn, argues that at least he did not rape someone's little child. Each prisoner is failing to identify himself with an ideal type criminal. In a sense, he is therefore identifying himself as a noncriminal.

It is a fact that we now can embezzle without thinking of ourselves as crooks—"The robber is the real criminal; I am just an unfortunate businessman that got caught short." Embezzlement rates would go down drastically if we could somehow convince ourselves and our trusted employees that anyone who violates his position of trust must necessarily identify himself as a thief, not as a "borrower" or some other nice kind of person.

A sound set of sociological theory enables us to predict that people will identify themselves with an ideal type if they are officially handled as if they are members of the ideal type, and if they have intimate association with those who conceive of themselves as members of the ideal type. Thus, a boy who steals a car and is officially handled as a criminal is much more likely to think of himself as a criminal than is a boy who steals a car and is merely reprimanded by the victim. Similarly, a criminal who associates intimately with other criminals who might be proud of the fact that they are criminals, such as professional thieves, is likely to think of himself as a criminal. And a man who is handled as an anti-thief and who has intimate association with anti-thieves will identify himself strongly as an anti-thief. Now, trusted persons can only with very great difficulty picture themselves as embezzlers, because the popular stereotype does not fit them. They, therefore, cannot be anti-embezzlers. What I am proposing is an educational program that calls a spade a spade. That is, we need programs in which we say over and over again that a person that "pilfers" or "taps the till" or "borrows" or who is guilty of "defalcation," "peculation," or some other nice term of this kind is, in fact, a crook.

In summary, then, it is my belief that embezzlement requires a nonshareable need, a position of trust and a knowledge of how it can be misused, and a verbal rationalization that allows the embezzler to avoid seeing himself as a thief. Regardless of the systems which can be arranged to reduce opportunity, the perfect system of internal control has never been invented, and probably never will be. No matter what the degree of restriction imposed upon trusted persons in modern business, an element of trust must always remain. An attention to morale and employee problems is a most direct contribution to reducing nonshareable problems, while continuing company programs and attitudes about theft can go far toward preventing the type of verbal "escape" which the embezzler uses to excuse himself.

Donald R. Cressey

Dr. Cressey is Professor of Sociology at the University of California, Santa Barbara. He joined the Department of Anthropology-Sociology at UCLA in 1949. After moving through the ranks of professorship at UCLA, Professor Cressey moved to the Santa Barbara campus, where he served from 1962-1967 as Dean of the College of Letters and Sciences. Since 1967, he has been engaged in full-time teaching, research, and public service.

An international authority on the sociology of delinquency, crime, criminal justice, and corrections, Professor Cressey has conducted research in five prisons, a police department, a probation-parole agency, a prosecuting attorney's office, and in several juvenile courts. His research has been honored by prizes from the Illinois Academy of Criminology and the American Society of Criminology.

In addition to many articles in professional journals, Professor Cressey has published nine books. Principles of Criminology *went into its ninth edition in 1974.* Theft of the Nation: The Structure and Operations of Organized Crime in America *(1969) is based on work Dr. Cressey did while a special consultant for President Johnson's Commission on Law Enforcement and Administration of Justice. His first book,* Other People's Money: A Study in the Social Psychology of Embezzlement *(1953) was recently reissued.*

Chapter 7

CUTTING EMBEZZLEMENT LOSSES

(The following is excerpted from the foreword and conclusion of a pamphlet, "How to Reduce Embezzlement Losses," published by Royal-Globe Insurance Companies in 1968.)

No one can assure that proper treatment of employees and realistic internal controls will defeat embezzlement although we do know they will *reduce the possibility* of occurrence materially. To protect itself to the greatest degree, a concern must give heed not only to those areas, but provide for detailed audits and a sound bonding program as well. Auditors will be able to make suggestions regarding the scope of audit needed and to detect breakdowns in the system of controls. A bond will serve as a necessary supplement to the systems, for no procedures have ever been devised to guarantee the prevention of embezzlement and it is doubtful that there will ever be.

© 1968 by Royal-Globe Insurance Companies. Reprinted by permission. Requests for copies of "How to Reduce Embezzlement Losses" should be addressed to Mrs. L.E.B. Fuchs, Bond Dept., Royal-Globe Insurance Companies, 150 William St., New York, N.Y. 10038. Include $1.00 for each copy ordered.

It has been said that the only person who can take advantage of us is the person we trust, a highly accurate statement as respects embezzlers. Such trusted employees walk out each working day with more than $8,000,000 of their employers' cash and merchandise—a total of more than two billion dollars annually. This is many times the amount lost to burglars or robbers during 1967. It is sad to report, however, that no statistics are available to support these figures. The reader might ask "Why not? Don't insurance companies keep records of losses paid?" The answer is obvious; "We *do* keep records!" But, and here's the catch, it is estimated that only some 15% of eligible mercantile concerns have had the foresight to protect themselves against the contingency of employee dishonesty. For example, it would be unusual if one weren't aware of a fire in a neighbor's building or even within the community if for no other reason than the event would undoubtedly be recorded in the local newspaper. Conversely, it is a rare occurrence when, except for certain management personnel, employees are aware of an embezzlement even within their own concern—and only the larger losses appear in the press.

Actually, there are many who believe the two billion dollars lost by employee dishonesty each year to be a most conservative figure and virtually all underwriters of fidelity bonds or policies support this supposition. Dishonest employees reduce the profit an employee rightfully expects from his efforts. It must be remembered that, if a 5% profit is expected, some $200,000 worth of goods must be produced to compensate for each $10,000 lost through dishonesty.

Embezzled Merchandise

Through popular association, embezzlement has become almost synonymous with the misappropriation of money alone, but a substantial amount of the two billion dollar annual loss results from the wrongful conversion of merchandise as well. There are no accurate statistics to reveal cash versus merchandise losses, but some authorities have placed the value of the latter at seven times the former.

No class of merchandise can be deemed unattractive to the employee who is bent on dishonesty if he either can use it or find an outlet for it. Thus, a broom manufacturer was shocked to discover a $15,000 loss of his merchandise. Employees of a cardboard box manufacturer methodically removed more than $500,000 worth of these boxes over a period of years. A large drug manufacturer lost over $50,000 in non-narcotic pills to an employee who had sewn a bag inside his coat, filling the bag with the fruits of his labor each day as he left.

The businessman who relies upon his own conception of the stealability of his product to determine the extent to which it should be protected may be in for a rude awakening some black morning. "It can't happen to me, I *know* my people," has led more than one concern down the road to financial disaster.

The Embezzler

While much effort has been expended to develop an accurate picture of the criminal in general, few studies have been devoted to a specific crime such as embezzlement, so we must content ourselves with findings telling us little more than that the embezzler might be *anyone*.

He is likely to give the appearance of being a pillar of the community, enjoying the respect of his fellow workers and friends. The potential embezzler cannot be recognized as having distinctive physical attributes, living in a specific area, displaying identifying personality quirks, or emanating from a particular stratum of society. This *respectability* is probably the most common denominator of embezzlers and is the primary reason why the employer must ensure that adequate controls are established in all areas of his business.

The motivation or use to which the money is put and the method of abstracting the funds or merchandise, however, are not similar. In fact, it is not even a requisite that an embezzler must "profit" from his peculation. Fidelity underwriters have viewed many claims where the embezzler has obtained little or no tangible reward for the taking of funds or merchandise from his employer, but for reasons best left to the psychiatrist his dishonesty has permitted others to profit. The desire to exceed quotas, for example, might cause an employee to overstate his sales by manipulating records.

The observant employer, however, may be able to detect symptoms frequently exhibited by embezzlers and nip losses before they become damaging.

The primary symptom is a drastic change in spending habits, an increase in the employee's standard of living.

A second danger signal may be an employee's apparent devotion to his work. This is particularly true of the "trusted" employee who handles all aspects of transactions himself and who refuses to take vacations on the grounds he is "too busy." If anyone else were to perform his duties or if his access to other records were blocked, he might be unmasked.

A third symptom, which is actually another version of the second, is objection to procedural changes that would lead to closer supervision.

Elements of Embezzlement

The employer must have an appreciation of the elements of embezzlement if he intends to lessen the possibility of such loss to his concern. Generally we can expect that three elements must be present for an embezzlement to occur—need or desire, rationalization and opportunity. Following is a brief outline of these three elements and their components:

1.   *Need or Desire*—The motivation that plants the seeds of embezzlement may spring from any one of three sources.

First, the embezzler may have a problem which, according to his definition, is unshareable. For those who have delved into the problem this is the aspect accorded the greatest attention and, in fact, is the sole motivation according to many. Such a problem may arise from gambling, extravagant living standards, unusual family expenses, and inadequate income (unrealistic wage policy). There are other reasons, but those listed above are the most important.

The second source from which motivation is supplied is the psychological need of the embezzler. While this is not nearly as common as the unshareable problem, it does arise in a sufficient number of cases to justify comment. Examples of this might be: intense desire to succeed in employment, philanthropy (the modern Robin Hood who derives abnormal satisfaction from helping others—at the expense of his employer), dupery (the employee's need for pleasing, to be accepted, allows someone to knowingly take advantage of him), and revenge.

A third motivating source, one that cannot be ignored, is the criminal tendency within some employees. If embezzlement was not made so easy, employees in this category would probably turn to other forms of crime to appease their desires.

2.   *Rationalization*—Although need or desire for financial gain resides in an individual, most must justify their dishonest actions to themselves in order to avoid creating anxiety. Anxiety will arise from the conflict introduced by committing an act he recognizes as wrong. The burglar or robber, once the overt act is committed, leaves the location of the crime hopeful that he will not be discovered. Conversely, the embezzler must "live" with his actions on a day-to-day basis—thus the importance of this rationalization.

Primarily, such rationalizations will be found in: *borrowing* (the employee will convince himself he is merely "using" the funds temporarily and will replace them as soon as possible. He, therefore, will not conceive of himself as a "thief"); *moral right* (the defaulter may feel he is underpaid and reasons that he is entitled to greater compensation); *lack of moral restraint* (the employee may see others stealing and getting away with it and therefore feels he is merely doing what everyone else is doing); and *reward within the group* (the desire to steal being instilled by others with success in such criminal activity encountering no social disapproval). There are other rationalizations, but these listed are predominant.

3.   *Opportunity*—Management alone is responsible for this element of the embezzlement syndrome. It is afforded by *omissions of controls, inadequacy of established controls.* Without opportunity, regardless of the strength or importance of the first two elements, an embezzlement cannot occur.

Reducing the Elements

Reasonable effort by management can make *need and desire* less likely to arise. While enlightened management might lessen the desire element, need cannot be influenced to the same extent as it is not subject to the same degree of control by management. For example, an employee adequately compensated for his position with an annual salary of $10,000 might *need* $20,000 (or more) because of the unshareable problem we previously mentioned.

Rationalization is the most nebulous element of the three we have discussed because generally it is an interpretation the employee makes of the situation and his conception of his actions. Management, however, can take several steps to make the employee's ability to reconcile his actions more difficult. Employees can be made conscious of management's attitude towards embezzlement and dishonest employees during the pre-employment interviews, and continual reminders can be given through posters or periodic bulletins. Management must be as willing to remind employees of their intent and desire to prevent embezzlement as they are to prevent accidents. When visiting a plant we often note signs advising of how many work days are lost because of accidents. How often do we see advices stating thievery has cost a plant a certain amount of profits? Audits and internal spot-checks by management will make it more difficult for an employee to justify his position. These will assist in making the employee aware of management's attitude and thus will be another factor in the elimination of rationalization.

Opportunity, the third element required for the occurrence of an embezzlement, lends itself to control by management more readily than either of the other two. In spite of this, it is management's inattention to this aspect that permits losses to reach their astronomical annual level. Management can take measures to modify need and desire, to block the embezzler's avenues of rationalization, but there can be no substitute for good internal controls designed to minimize opportunity.

The keynote of realistic controls is the segregation of duties so that no *one* employee will be responsible for (1) handling funds and maintaining sole records thereof, or (2) handling merchandise and maintaining sole records thereof. Where personnel is limited, the work of employees whose duties cannot be segregated must be given closer attention by management.

Collusion

Collusive possibilities must also be recognized by management. Many of the questions which at first blush may appear superfluous have been designed to combat collusion to some degree. Next to losses caused by lone wolf embezzlers who are able to perpetrate them by virtue of their handling transactions from start to finish, collusion is the major cause of catastrophic losses.

The establishment of adequate internal controls is not only important to owners of a business, but employers also have a moral responsibility to eliminate temptation from the potential embezzler.

The embezzler is one of the most pathetic of all criminals. He often starts with small peculations to tide him over a financially rough spot, feeling he can replace what is taken before it is missed. More funds invariably become necessary before he can make restitution, so more is taken. Before long he becomes entangled in a situation from which he seemingly cannot extricate himself by more conventional means and he may turn to gambling to recoup the funds taken previously. But this requires additional financing. More of the employer's funds are used to finance this venture. With the odds against him, it is doubtful the embezzler finds this a successful solution, thus further attempts are made which also fail. Finally, the loss becomes so large that it cannot be concealed and he is unmasked.

This normally will prove to be fleeting relief, however, as his problems generally multiply following disclosure. Employers who have the foresight to investigate the background of applicants may be reluctant to hire him, his family may be held up to ridicule or he may be incarcerated. Property may have to be sold to make restitution, his wife might have to seek employment instead of devoting her full time to homemaking. The family's standard of living undoubtedly will be lowered and children may be prevented from entering or continuing in higher education.

If such a tragic happening can be prevented through proper treatment of employees or control over their duties before the embezzlement occurs, it should be.

* * *

For more than 120 years, Royal-Globe Insurance Companies has been a leading property-casualty insurer in the United States. The firm offers a complete range of property, liability, fidelity, surety, marine, aviation and life insurance.

Royal-Globe operates in all 50 states, and is part of one of the largest international insurance groups, conducting operations in more than 80 countries and writing policies in 16 languages.

Chapter 8

EMBEZZLEMENT BY COMPUTER

By Alan Adelson

"I could steal a company blind in three months and leave its books looking balanced," boasts Sheldon Dansiger, a burly, 33-year-old data processing specialist.

His methods: Electronic embezzlement. His accomplice: The company's own computer.

Increasingly, business transactions that formerly were recorded on ledger pages are being translated into magnetic impulses in a computer's memory section. It's a simple matter for a crook with technical know-how and a little imagination to program a computer to fleece a company and fool its auditors, according to Mr. Dansiger.

He says corporate executives rarely question the reliability of financial results that emerge from complex million-dollar machines. "They simply forget that the machines have been built to do whatever the operators direct," explains Mr. Dansiger. "There's nothing to stop them from working quite efficiently for a crook."

© 1968, 1975, Security World Publishing Co., Inc.

Missing Money

Joseph J. Wasserman, who heads a Bell Telephone Laboratories task force seeking to devise methods of auditing computers used by the Bell System, says many companies already have been hit with heavy losses, but their managements don't know it. He predicts that within a few years someone will uncover a computerized embezzlement that will make even the $150 million salad oil swindle seem puny.

Computers are operating faster and faster and producing fewer and fewer of the printouts that auditors and financial officers need to follow the flow of dollars processed by the machines. "If auditing staffs don't get involved in designing computer systems soon, they might as well climb up on their stools, pull down their green eyeshades, and pray for retirement to come," says Mr. Wasserman.

Others who are aware of the growing problem echo the sentiments of Messrs. Dansiger and Wasserman. "If I were a crook, I'd work through computers," asserts Robert Fano, a leading computer theoretician at Massachusetts Institute of Technology. Ralph Salerno, a former New York City detective who is now a member of a state committee investigating organized crime in New York, says: "I'm not a gambling man, but if I were, I'd bet a month's pay that the Mafia will be working with computers in a few years."

Bilking A Broker

A number of electronic embezzlements already have come to light. The manager in charge of back-office operations at Walston & Co., a New York brokerage firm, electronically siphoned $250,000 out of the company between 1951 and 1959. By the time the theft was uncovered, the man had become a vice president.

He programmed Walston's computer to transfer money from a company account to two customers' accounts—his and his wife's. The computer was further programmed to show the money had gone to purchase stock for the two accounts. Then he sold the stock supposedly purchased, pocketed the cash and transferred some more.

When a Walston official sensed something was amiss, an examination of the two accounts revealed major irregularities. But the company could not figure out the embezzler's system. Because he hadn't stolen any money from customers' accounts, "what he did was absolutely undetectable without internal auditing," says William D. Fleming, Walston president. "Before it happened no one dreamed such a thing was possible, and if he hadn't explained how he did it, we probably still wouldn't know."

The thief explained to Walston's incredulous directors that he pulled off the elaborate money swap by going into the office early Sunday mornings to punch new computer cards and feed them into the machines. "It took someone with absolute knowledge of the computer system to do it," says Mr. Fleming. "This guy was the boss back there. He set up the system and ran the whole show."

"Anyone Could Do It"

Walston recovered only a fraction of the stolen money. The firm promptly revamped its computer system, instituting a quarterly internal audit and other safeguards designed to foil embezzlement attempts. The former vice president served a year in Sing Sing prison and is now a furniture salesman.

Even as the Walston theft was being uncovered, a similar embezzlement was beginning at another New York brokerage firm, Carlisle & Jacquelin. From 1959 to 1963, the firm's data processing manager got away with $81,120 by instructing a computer to write checks to fictitious persons and send them to his home address. The scheme was uncovered when the Post Office accidentally returned one of the checks to the firm and the clerk who received it became suspicious.

George Muller, a managing partner of Carlisle & Jacquelin, refused to discuss the case. "We'd have to be crazy to give out all the details now so that anyone who wanted to could do it again," says Mr. Muller. Court records show that the embezzler was convicted, returned the money and received a suspended sentence.

More recently, National City Bank of Minneapolis discovered that the employee programming the computerized check-handling system it set up in 1965 embezzled $1,357 over a period of about a year. He programmed the computer to completely disregard his personal checks any time his account had insufficient funds to cover them. The computer allowed each of his bad checks to clear the bank and didn't debit the employee's account for the over-drafts.

The scheme was discovered only by accident, when a computer breakdown forced hand-processing of some checks. One of the embezzler's bad checks bounced. When bank officials confronted him, the employee readily disclosed his scheme. The ex-employee later pleaded guilty, repaid the money and received a suspended sentence.

Computer specialists tell of other ways employees can program computers to steal for them. A crook can change one figure in a computer program, and the machine will report abnormally high inventory losses as normal merchandise breakage, enabling accomplices to steal vast amounts of goods from warehouses without the theft being noticed. Later the operator can remove the evidence by putting the original figure back into the computer program.

Computerized payroll systems are potential bonanzas for embezzlers, the experts say. A computer operator can create paychecks for fictitious employees and pay extra overtime and wages to himself quite simply. If he's more ambitious, he can program the computer to deduct a few extra pennies of "income tax" from every paycheck in the plant and pay himself the amount collected.

Unsafe Safeguards

It's possible to program some safeguards against embezzlement into computers, the specialists say, but the process is complicated and costly and sometimes involves entirely rewriting computer programs and shutting down the machines for a time. Adding safeguards "will cost a company money, and the temptation is often to economize," says Roy Freed, counsel for the computer control division of Honeywell, Inc.

But even the most elaborate safeguards might not foil a skilled embezzler. There's always the danger that a crook will come along who's more clever than the specialists who programmed the safeguards into the computer. Lloyd McChesney, chief examiner for the New York Stock Exchange, says that although member firms recently tightened their computer auditing procedures, "no one has yet developed a way to keep his books with a 100% guarantee against embezzlements."

Data processing specialists, however, say there are a few basic rules company officials can follow at least to make it more difficult for a computer crook to raid the corporate treasury.

A cardinal rule, according to the specialists: Don't let the computer programmer actually operate the machine. A crook who can build a loophole into the system and also feed it the data necessary to carry out his embezzlement scheme is more likely to succeed than a crook who, after programming the machine, must sit back and hope another operator will innocently let the machine divert funds to him.

Computer Sleuthing

Manuel Stonewood—who, with Mr. Dansiger, operates a New York management consulting and "computer sleuthing" firm called EDP Associates Inc.—says he passed up some golden opportunities to steal large sums from a major New York City bank not long ago. "I alone designed a mutual fund's dividend system for the bank, wrote the program for it, then ran the job on the computer," says Mr. Stonewood.

"The operation was so big it had a mistake tolerance of several hundred thousand dollars," claims Mr. Stonewood. "I could have paid at least half that much to myself in small checks if I had been so inclined, and the money wouldn't have been missed."

A second rule recommended by the specialists: Segregate computerized check-writing operations from the departments that authorize checks. This setup makes it difficult for an embezzler to convert fudged data into actual cash pay-outs. And it makes it easier for management to spot checks issued by a computer that has been tampered with.

Another rule: Transfer computer programmers and operators frequently to different machines and different programs. The theory is that if a crook knows he won't be working on a single job long enough to bilk it for large sums, he's less likely to go to the trouble of rigging the computer to steal. Even if he does rig it, the next man on that job may spot the embezzlement procedure.

Computer Auditing Techniques

What such safeguards fail to prevent, auditors are supposed to catch, of course. But many data processing specialists say most auditors don't understand computers, so a clever embezzler can fool them. Some large accounting firms have developed their own highly skilled staffs of computer auditors, but even these specialists can be deceived because so much of what goes on inside the machine never appears on a computer print-out.

"Unless you built right into the system a means of printing out audit information, you aren't going to get readable financial records anymore," says Mr. Wasserman of Bell Labs. He says his team of specialists already has developed several new computer auditing techniques that might eventually be used throughout the Bell System.

One technique involves programming a computer to spot seeming irregularities in operating procedures and immediately print out a copy of the questionable transaction for auditors to examine. Another method involves feeding test data into the computer and then checking to determine whether anything interfered with proper processing.

Mr. Wasserman says the Bell System's auditing setup will do far more than spot crooks. For one thing, it will alert executives more quickly to fluctuations in overtime costs, inventory changes and other areas that can have an immediate impact on corporate profits. He says computers currently are used to check the efficiency of telephone operators and to audit employees' calls to guard against widespread misuse of long-distance equipment.

Chapter 9

EXECUTIVE DISHONESTY:
MISUSE OF AUTHORITY FOR PERSONAL GAIN

By Ronald R. Schmidt

When I looked for a dictionary definition of executive dishonesty, I was not surprised to find there was none. I've come up with my own definition of executive dishonesty as "the misuse of authority for personal gain, to the detriment of an organization." This definition does not limit the subject to presidents, vice presidents, and chairmen of the board; it encompasses anyone who exercises authority over others in making decisions that could adversely affect the company.

This could include a chairman of the board or president who becomes involved in the manipulation of stocks for personal gain; it could include a vice president of personnel who hires an unqualified relative or friend; it could include a purchasing agent who accepts an inferior product at a higher price to receive a kickback; or it could include a shipping foreman who orders an employee to overload a truck knowing that he's going to split the proceeds of this overload with the driver.

Not all acts of executive dishonesty involve thievery. Some in-

From a presentation given at the International Security Conference in Chicago, 1971.

volve sheer negligence in the performance of duty. In the example above of the vice president of personnel, his personal gain was the favor or friendship he gained from hiring an unqualified individual. Regardless of how we categorize these acts, they have one common denominator: Each one affects the bottom line of the profit and loss statement and results in a loss to the company involved.

The security director or security manager may feel that these areas are outside of his responsibilities. He is responsible for proper fencing, employee ID cards, lunch-box inspections, and so on. The definition of security varies from one person to another. To some, it could mean a substantial bank account, or a new insurance policy, or warships protecting our coastal areas. It could be a policeman walking his beat. These different concepts of security share one common denominator: Security means making safe that which we hold to be of value.

By this definition, we find that any act for some form of personal gain that is detrimental to the company falls within the realm of security. For the most part, we will be concerned with dishonest acts by executives that result in monetary gains; but the security director should also work to establish lines of communication that will help him discuss, investigate, and recommend solutions for other forms of dishonesty that could be robbing his company of much-deserved profits.

Losses Staggering

It is significant that while rank-and-file employees are responsible for a large number of internal thefts, the major dollar loss in business and industry is attributed to the acts of the dishonest executive. Many of the losses that result from one dishonest act by an executive run $50,000, $100,000 and more. Some "best guess" estimates indicate that on-the-take executives are siphoning off more than 5 billion dollars a year. This is a sum higher than the cost of embezzlement and non-executive employee thievery put together.

The inability to resist temptation is as old as man himself. Likewise, man's desire to investigate is not new. In the Old Testament, Numbers 13, Moses sent scouts to bring back reports on the land of Canaan. Moses appreciated the value of being completely informed on important matters. The reports that he received, however, were conflicting, and this problem continues to plague businessmen today. They don't get all the facts as to where business losses are actually occurring.

The dishonest person could live in any state in the country, in a large city or small town. He may be employed in any business, industry, financial institution, or he could be a public official. He could hold any position from chairman of the board to junior third-shift cleanup man. It isn't necessary that he handle money. If he is intent on being dishonest, he will find the opportunity to act on that intent. According to management consultants who specialize in executive dishonesty, there is a better than even chance of sizable dishonesty in any company at any given time.

Toleration of Executive Dishonesty

Many people tend to be tolerant of the dishonest executive because they don't feel personally threatened by him. One of the reasons for this is that the executive seldom has to resort to acts of force or violence to get what he wants. The victim of his crime is usually an impersonal company or large corporation. Many people feel, therefore, that as individuals they are in no danger whatsoever from him. What they fail to consider, of course, is that dishonest executives take money from all of us in the form of higher prices for products and services.

The dishonest executive is frequently a member of the middle or upper class. Often he is college educated and has been exposed to all the ethical values that Western civilization holds dear. Above all, he does not consider himself to be a criminal.

Let's take a look at an active day in the life of a dishonest executive. During the day, he bribes a police officer and a building inspector who is working on his new plan. He cheats on his income tax. He entertains his wife at the company's expense. He accepts a kickback in the form of a color TV set. He juggles his books. He issues a misleading advertisement. He pockets an office set for his personal use, and he tells his wife to forget about the maid's Social Security tax.

That evening, like you and me, he goes home and sits down to read the newspaper. Reading about holdups, robberies, and other acts of thievery, he turns to his wife and says, "What's this world coming to with all this crime?" The truth is, had that executive been successfully prosecuted for each of his illegal acts during that day, he could have received a long jail sentence and a large fine.

Precautions Limit Temptation

Let's take a look at some of the reasons for executive dishonesty. Man's inability to resist temptation dates back to Adam and Eve. Given the necessary circumstances, nearly any man may be tempted to steal. Whether or not he will yield to temptation cannot be totally determined in advance. Studies have found that 30%—3 out of every 10 people—will not steal regardless of the need or regardless of the opportunity. The studies also reveal that another 40% will not become involved in acts of thievery if reasonable security precautions have been taken. (Reasonable security precautions include locks and plate glass windows, for example.) But the remaining 30% will actually seek out and create the opportunity to engage in thievery.

An actual case history will point out how these figures bear out in some real situations. I will not mention this firm's name, but it was a large firm with 1,400 employees across the country. They had an inventory shrinkage up in the millions of dollars. The company decided to try to pinpoint where the loss was occurring. What they decided to do was to call in each of the 1,400 employees individually and say, "John, we have a bit of a problem. You've been with us now for ten years. Last year we had an inventory shrinkage up in the millions. If we can find out where this loss is occurring, we can set up effective means to prevent it from happening again. So we'd like to ask your help. If you've stolen more than one hundred dollars' worth of our products within the last year, we'd like you to confess to it. We won't write anything down; we won't put anything in your personnel record. You will continue your job and nothing will be held against you. By the same token, John, if you tell us you didn't take anything, we're going to ask you to take a polygraph examination. If it indicates that you were lying to us and that in fact you did steal more than $100, we're going to dismiss you. Do you agree to that?" John answers, "Fine."

They went through the 1,400 employees, and 62% or 868 confessed to taking more than $100 worth of goods in the last year. They ran polygraph tests, and the figure jumped up to 76% or 1,064.

Motives to steal may grow out of any one of a whole range of human emotions, ambitions, difficulties, desires. The traditional causes, and those which appeal to the public imagination, are sometimes called the three R's: rum, redheads, and racing. A fourth cause, gaining prominence within the last few years, is drug addiction. And, of course, there are less dramatic reasons, such as the expense of keeping up with the neighbors, or operating a small business on the side, or heavy medical expenses, or just the general feeling of the need to get even with the company for a real or imaginary wrong.

Dishonesty Rises During Business Slump

The number of dishonest acts coming to light has risen alarmingly during the prolonged business slump that we've been experiencing. This is for two reasons: 1) Unemployment, shrinking paychecks, career setbacks, stock market losses, and other personal misfortunes have increased during the business slump. 2) The recession has brought to light a surprising number of dishonest acts that had gone undetected while business was booming. In prosperous times the rising sales and profits often mask what's really going on, so that a dishonest executive does not get caught until business turns bad and he can no longer manipulate the figures to conceal his thefts.

An example of this is a top executive who borrowed $60,000 from a bank to take advantage of a stock option that was running out. When the value of his shares dropped to less than half of the original purchase price, the bank started pounding on his door to recall the loan, and he became a bit panicky. He wasn't content just to get the $60,000 back and pay off the loan. He got used to that easy money. Greed set in, and he continued. He clipped them for $150,000 in kickbacks before he was caught, in less than a year.

As a result of the business slowdown, there have also been cases uncovered of executives who submitted exaggerated sales and profit figures to win bonuses and promotions for themselves. In one case, a retail firm had to request a refund from the Internal Revenue Service of $1 million that had been paid on non-existent profits reported by one of their divisional managers. In this case, the man did not do it for his personal gain; he was not getting any bonus but wanted to make himself look good.

In another case, a top executive clipped over $400,000 from his company by submitting trucking and storage bills. This was a collusion type of theft which involved an accomplice in the shipping department and an outside independent trucking firm.

In another recent case, auditors discovered a $50,000 inventory shortage in the camera department of one store of a large discount chain. The shortage was incurred in a five-month period. Working on a 2.5 business/profit ratio, the management of this firm was cautioned that if the loss rate continued, they would have to sell an extra $4,000 worth of camera equipment to cover every $100 worth of camera equipment that was stolen, just to break even.

This was a complex investigation involving undercover work, outside investigation, surveillance, and interrogation. What the team of investigators uncovered was staggering in scope. The assistant manager was charging admission for obscene films shown in the store after hours, using the store's equipment. He was working in collusion with a salesman in the store; merchandise was regularly being removed. The assistant manager and the salesman also conspired with employees in other departments to arrange similar deals. It turned out that employees in practically every department of the store were stealing merchandise and trading it with other departments. The manager of the store was aware of the theft but couldn't say anything because he was also involved.

Investigation of the assistant manager disclosed that he was a heavy gambler. He was working under an assumed name, with an assumed address, and had been bonded under these conditions. He was married and the father of three, but was involved with an employee of the store. He had been dismissed from several previous jobs for suspected theft. It also turned out that the assistant manager was the cousin of the salesman he was in collusion with, and the salesman had a lengthy police record for similar activities.

Violation of Trust

The essential difference between executive dishonesty and "rank-and-file" dishonesty is that executive dishonesty is always related to a violation of trust connected with the position. What makes this so important is the moral issue involved. Many dishonest acts by executives attack the fundamental principles of American business. The same act committed by an employee not in a position of trust does not have the same impact. A doctor who performs an illegal abortion and gets caught makes headlines. What happens when a midwife performs an abortion? It may appear in a back corner of the newspaper. When the pharmacist is caught dispensing narcotics illegally it makes headlines. When Joe, the hippie, gets caught, it gets little notice. The actions of the doctor and pharmacist represent violations of trust; the others do not. This is the same principle we're talking about when an executive who is entrusted with his position in a company violates that position; this is a case of executive dishonesty.

Unlike the rank-and-file dishonest employee, the dishonest executive does not have to hide tools in his lunch box or throw tires over a fence for a later pickup, or break into the petty cash box. He probably has the keys to the building to begin with; he has access to the items desired and can probably change the records to cover up the loss.

More Than Physical Security Needed

We must remember that controls in a business are not solely a matter of locking up doors and examining packages. We must go deeper than the physical problem. Dishonesty is a problem in human relations, and top management's attitudes and policies contribute to this problem. In order for a high, ethical standard to be maintained, top management must set the example. If they fail to do so, all the employees will adopt an attitude of "they don't care; why should I?"

Some security personnel may not believe that these problems exist in their companies. Unfortunately, past experience has shown that the odds would be in our favor if we were to bet to the contrary. Let's take a look at some basic facts. Number one, all employees, including executives, are susceptible to temptation. Number two, temptations in the form of opportunities to steal money or other valuable properties exist in almost every business, and especially so for the executive. Number three, stealing by executives is estimated to run to $5 billion a year. Number four, dishonest employees, especially executives, defy detection. They don't, for one minute, expect to be caught. That's what makes it such a dangerous risk to a company and why losses often reach such sizable proportions before being discovered. Number five, there is no such thing as a theft-proof accounting system.

Security personnel must accept these facts as basic; and in so doing they must also recognize that these facts cover all employees of a business, from the top down. The security officer's responsibility is to the company as a whole. It does not cease with the hourly-rated personnel, nor does it cease with the lower echelon salaried personnel. It continues right up the ladder and includes all personnel regardless of their superior or subordinate positions. With this awareness established, security should then set its sights towards establishing effective means to reduce the risks of an executive becoming dishonest.

Standard Methods of Loss Control

Even those who have been in the security business only a short time should have learned the importance of improved personnel selection in the control of loss. This includes a detailed employment application and an in-depth investigation to establish the validity of the information on the application. This should not end with the mere confirmation of employment dates and last salary. It should continue with searching questions as to attitude, achievements, responsibilities, accomplishments, living standards, and circumstances under which the employee left his previous jobs.

Another standard method of loss control, of course, is division of responsibility, thus limiting the authority of any one individual. For example, a credit manager should not be permitted to receive money and at the same time be charged with the posting and depositing and preparation and distribution of monthly statements to clients.

The third standard method is to have periodic audits and reviews performed by outside auditors. The people who are being checked should not be asked to do the audit themselves. Controls and regular inventories are also important; the reconciliation of bank statements, the posting of cash receipts, cash disbursements, and general ledgers all help control losses.

Another key method is to have all personnel bonded. Many businessmen are still unaware of the psychological as well as financial benefits derived from bonding employees. Less than 15% of the companies victimized by dishonest executives are covered by a fidelity bond. This is true despite the fact that experience has shown that executives who know they are bonded are less likely to steal than those who are not bonded. Some organizations, of course, find it difficult or impossible to obtain fidelity bonds on their employees. In fact, the largest carrier of honesty bond coverage in this country will not bond banks and other financial institutions that have been in business for less than six years. The risk is too great. The banker himself, who once feared the bank robber, now says, "I can handle bank robbers; it's the trusted employees I'm worried about."

Some companies, of course, may follow all of these standard methods of loss control and yet still become the victims of executive dishonesty. Because of that percentage of the population who will seek and create opportunities for theft, some losses are inevitable. They can be minimized, but they will occur. Adherence to these standard methods of pre-employment screening, honesty bond coverage and so on will serve to keep honest that 40% who will not become involved in acts of thievery if reasonable security precautions have been taken. And it will also serve to discover a loss more expediently when it does occur. It is disheartening to read of a 28-year employee who was caught stealing and admitted he had been stealing since the day he started with the firm. It took 28 years for the company to catch him. Had these procedures been followed, chances are he would have been detected in six months or a year.

Warning Signs of Dishonesty

What are some of the signs and signals of executive dishonesty? The most common reply to this question is to be alert for employees apparently living beyond their means; especially those making $25,000 a year or less. This answer, however, for the most part does not suffice for the top level executive, as expensive habits are harder to detect since his salary already entitles him to a high standard of living.

Of course, there are exceptions. In one case a top executive who was making well over $25,000 was discovered, rather accidentally, to be on the take. One day a telephone call came in in his absence, and somebody intercepted it. The call concerned his proposed purchase of a $200,000 island in the Bahamas. You don't have to be too smart to figure out that even if he were making $40,000 a year, it would be pretty tough to afford an island in the Bahamas.

Experience has shown that in the majority of cases the money derived from dishonest acts is considered "easy money." The old adage "easy come, easy go" may have come about because of early acts of theft. Continued experience has proved that an overwhelming percentage of dishonest executives use the money they obtain dishonestly for some form of purchase or investment. Very seldom is that money stuck in a shoe box or a safety deposit box.

Another very alarming signal could come from a firm's quality control department. If there are frequent complaints about the quality of materials used in the manufacture of products, and the purchasing department keeps on buying these materials, this calls for an investigation. Of course, the absence of such complaints does not mean there is no problem. They may be buying quality materials, but in excessive amounts to cover the kickback. To curb this possibility, the suppliers' bids should be reviewed continually and checked against the company's current market trends.

Companies that produce food products or other types of consumable items and have an employee purchase program should frequently check sales records for a noticeable absence of purchases made by people in a position to get a particular product.

Another potential red flag is the controller, credit manager, or head of a financial department who never takes a vacation. How many times have we read about the bookkeeper who never took a day off for 28 years, who finally caught the flu and was discovered to be an embezzler. Vacations for people in these positions should be insisted on, and someone else should perform their work in their absence.

Other "Sins" Cause Loss

Although executive theft is an important cause of loss, it is only one of the "seven-on-the-job sins" which siphon off a company's profits in bits and pieces. The other six sins are: lax supervision; time clock irregularities; safety violations; on-the-job gambling; sabotage; and waste. It is true that these "sins" are committed by rank-and-file employees, but many times they are committed with the knowledge of supervisors. By allowing these practices to occur without appropriate action, the supervisor becomes an accessory to the sin and therefore misuses his authority.

Several case histories may help to clarify this point. Lax supervision is usually a reflection of poor employee morale and indifference to management's objectives and policies. One case involved a casting and plating plant which manufactured various chrome trim items for the major auto manufacturers. The entire operation was at one plant covering the casting, buffing, plating, packaging, and shipping. The company was suffering large losses. An undercover investigator was assigned to the second shift as part of an eight-man cleanup crew. On his first night, one of his jobs was to clean up a machine where door handles were buffed before being wrapped and packaged. During an eight-hour shift the buffing compound residue would build up six inches high underneath the machine. The undercover man's job was to clean up this residue. Noticing door handles sticking helter-skelter out of the residue, the investigator got down on his hands and knees and started picking up the handles. The foreman came along and told him, "We don't have time for that; sweep everything out the door and into the hopper."

As it subsequently turned out, they had thrown about 600 pounds of finished, chrome-plated, polished, buffed door handles away that very day. The same foreman was responsible for the cleanup crew down the line on various other items the company manufactured. They had been losing over $25,000 a month in finished products, all because of waste and lax supervision. A contract disposal firm came in every day to pick up the large hoppers of waste. They were making a nice profit selling those door handles as scrap. Although all the elements of a collusion-type theft existed here, such was not found to be the case. It was sheer lack of supervision and negligence on the executive's part. This investigation continued for several months, during which time many other on-the-job sins were found in evidence.

Time-clock irregularities are also frequently committed with the supervisor's knowledge. We all know of cases where one individual will punch two time cards to cover up for a friend arriving late, perhaps not showing up at all, or leaving early. We've also had many cases of a man punching in, working an hour or two and then leaving, then returning at the end of the shift and punching out. The classic case that comes to mind concerns an undercover investigator assigned to the 3 p.m. to 11 p.m. second shift, working at a stamp machine. On this first day on the job, a fellow came up to him at about 8 o'clock and handed him 22 time cards and said, "Our policy here is that the low man on seniority punches out for everyone." As the evening progressed, fewer and fewer workers remained. By 11 o'clock, the only man left in the plant was the investigator. Even a foreman had left.

Surveillance the following night determined that some of the men had departed as much as five hours before the end of the shift. This on-the-job sin was committed with the knowledge of the foreman who was there to administer and manage affairs. And that's the definition of an executive—one who administers and manages affairs. His failure to meet these responsibilities made him a dishonest executive.

On-the-job gambling is also costly for a company. To begin with, it takes the employees away from their jobs for dice, cards, horse betting, and other games of chance. Many undercover men have witnessed plant and office card games where a single pot is larger than the weekly salary of any man in the game. This may be fine for the winner, but what about the loser? He has a problem of pure survival. One of the basic factors in a theft problem, of course, is need. The need for the bookkeeper or the purchasing agent to pay his rent or buy food for the family can become so great that he is going to succumb to any temptation that he can take advantage of. That opportunity could very well be company property.

Full Protection Needed

To place controls on only a portion of a company's vulnerable areas is not sufficient; any area left uncovered could result in the loss of deserved profits. The firm that does not take the necessary precautions with executive personnel will find competition selling at far less and showing a bigger profit. The members of management responsible for security are in a position to determine which side of the fence their company will be on.

Ronald R. Schmidt

Mr. Schmidt is Director of Security and Assistant Vice President of Pinkerton's, Inc. in New York City. He is responsible for operation and supervision of a security force of over 38,000 uniformed guards in the U.S. and Canada.

After joining Pinkerton's as an investigator in 1960, Mr. Schmidt opened the agency's Grand Rapids, Michigan office in 1965. Three years later he was reassigned as manager of the Chicago office. In 1970 he became Assistant Director, Department of Investigations, monitoring the investigative activities for 102 offices.

Mr. Schmidt's introduction to security and investigation came during five years of service with the U.S. Marine Corps, where he held various positions in Combat Intelligence, Air Intelligence and Counter Intelligence.

Section Two:
INVESTIGATING
INTERNAL THEFT

IV.
UNDERCOVER
INVESTIGATION

Chapter 10

UNDERCOVER INVESTIGATION
IN BUSINESS AND INDUSTRY

By Nathan T. Glaser

Security today is an essential part of business. The virtue of honesty has lost its status. Today there is more stealing by employees than ever before. A national magazine article on employee theft pictured 50 ways employees can steal, dramatizing the need for security. In the past three years, we at Merit have detected more dishonest employees than in any other three-year period of our fifty years of existence. These comments refer not to shoplifting, but mainly to employee fraud and theft in the retail and industrial fields.

Many Employee Thieves Are Young

Employees who are caught stealing average twenty years of age; many are much younger. Our files, of course, also show employees of long-time standing, who have had the confidence and trust of their employers, who have been discovered stealing. A 17-year-old youngster was recently caught stealing ten cartons of

From a presentation given at the International Security Conference in New York City, 1968.

cigarettes. He brazenly took them out of the store and put them in the trunk of his car. Not satisfied with the ten cartons, he repeated this act four times in one day. He confessed to stealing forty cartons of cigarettes, and there is no doubt he had done this many other times.

The next day an irate mother and father with their son in tow stormed the company's main office. The cry was: "Our son would never steal, and you got his confession under duress." We then questioned the boy over again, and he admitted to us, as he would not to his parents, that he had stolen this merchandise. While the mother and father were sitting there, we questioned him further about other merchandise he had taken, and he then admitted pilfering razor blades, lotions, and many more cartons of cigarettes.

Some punishment must be meted out to these young offenders. More publicity should be given by an organization when a person is apprehended. We cannot continue to let an employee who has committed a dishonest act go scot-free to be hired by another company.

Desire for Affluence as Motivation

Why are we detecting more dishonesty today than ever before? From my personal observations, having been in the field of security for many years and having interrogated thousands of employees, it appears that a desire for affluence has something to do with it. The idea that employers are comfortably well off makes some employees feel they also should have some of the benefits. Some of them feel they are not stealing; they are just taking something the company will not miss.

There are many reasons for employee theft. The cost of living has gone up, people are buying many major appliances on credit. They see others stealing and think, "Why shouldn't I?" Most importantly, management has made it too easy to steal.

What can we do to stop all this pilferage? This is the cry often heard from management. To answer this question, we must analyze some of the reasons for existing conditions.

Gap Between Management and Employees

Top level management is not getting a true picture of what is going on in their organizations today. The gap between top level management and the employees in their companies has been steadily widening. As growth and complexity in business increase, managers rely on their subordinate levels for reporting.

I am sure top management is sincere in their efforts to do the very best for their organizations. Employees are well-paid, with many fringe benefits. Management tries to provide a pleasant establishment and a safe place for employees to work in. They provide a means of livelihood for many people, who are expected to give a good day's work in return. The smart executive realizes that peak production comes from employees who are well-trained, well-supervised, and satisfied with their working conditions.

What makes a worker satisfied? Naturally, the benefits provided make a good start, but also important are proper training, clear instructions, and assistance and understanding in handling problems. Employees want fair treatment and, very importantly, recognition for excellence and dedication, as well as identity as trusted employees in their company.

However, many executives do not know if these conditions are being met. A supervisor is apt to report a rosy picture to his immediate superior when that picture is not so, because he himself may lack leadership or may be unfair in his actions and judgments.

What is management to do? The percentages of profits are off, inventory is off. Management may try to believe that the accountant or bookkeeper made an error in computation, but careful checking proves this is not so. Someone is stealing—but who, where and how? Management calls a meeting of key personnel to apprise them of the facts. They reply that, as far as they know, everything is running smoothly. . .more merchandise is being shipped, sales are increasing, people are working overtime, security is air-tight. They cannot imagine how anybody could be stealing.

This optimism is misleading. If management wants to know what is really going on in the business, there is only one sure way to find out: undercover investigation.

Value of Undercover Investigation

Our experience has shown that a professionally trained undercover operator from outside the business is the best way for the chief executive to bridge the communication gap between him and his people. This investigator will fit in as a regular employee. Management may find out that stealing, gambling, marijuana smoking are going on; that there is unnecessary overtime; employees are sleeping instead of working; supervisors are lax in their duties; no one is checking employees when they leave the place of business at lunch or closing time. The undercover operative can give management a picture of the morale in the company, as well as an evaluation of all employees, plus many more facts about the irritations that cause the serious decline of a business.

This means of security is invaluable. Its worth cannot be measured in dollars and cents. Undercover operations have actually saved a number of firms from going out of business.

As an illustration of some of the cases we've had, a large electrical firm was in financial difficulty despite good sales. During a lunch meeting, the firm's president told me of his problems and said he could not account for the fact they were losing money. I asked him if anyone knew he was having lunch with me; he said he had wanted his executive vice president to come with him, but he was out of town. I stressed the importance of not letting anyone, including the executive vice president, know. We arranged to place an undercover in his organization.

One week later one of the workers asked our undercover operative to help him load some electrical equipment and cables into his station wagon, as he had to make a delivery. When they finished loading the car, they drove directly to the executive vice president's home and deposited the merchandise in his garage. To make a long story short, when we interrogated this executive, he confessed to receiving over $150,000 worth of merchandise in this manner.

In another instance, after one of our engineers made a survey of a large variety chain, it was recommended that we place an undercover agent in their stock department. After a two-week period the manager solicited the help of our operator to deliver some merchandise for him that evening. It turned out that the manager also had a brother-in-law who had a variety store on the other side of town. They loaded a truck with merchandise from the company's warehouse and delivered it to the brother-in-law's establishment. The recovery in this case was very substantial.

Length of Investigation

When we contract with a client for an undercover assignment, the question is usually asked, "How long will it take?" Our minimum arrangement is eight weeks. During the first two weeks of that period, our operator will be given the opportunity to acclimate and familiarize himself with his environment. In the ensuing weeks he becomes very friendly with his co-workers. Of course, we may be able to complete an assignment before the eight weeks. However, we have one account on the books where our operator has been working constantly for over six years. On another account an operator has been working for over two years. Many operators have been working for over six months.

This may sound unusual, but these clients want a constant watch on their operation. Apprehensions have been made previously in all these organizations, but when we interrogate we do not break the agent's cover, thereby letting him continue work without suspicion.

In most jobs, the usual procedure is for one of our engineers to make a survey of the industrial plant or warehouse of the company. Where a retail store is involved, this is not necessary. The reason for the survey is to determine the most strategic area where an operator is needed. We check also for loopholes in an operation, such as exits, physical layouts, receiving and shipping departments, systems or procedures in billing, and so forth. We also determine from the client the days the salaries are paid, the type of personnel employed, and the problem they are mainly concerned with.

Detailed reports of our findings are mailed to the client's home each week. Nothing goes to the establishment, as these reports may fall into the wrong hands. We usually try to obtain the private telephone numbers of executives so that our calls do not go through a switchboard. All precautions are taken so that no one but the proper parties are aware that an undercover agent has been installed.

Qualifications of Undercover Operators

What makes a professional undercover operator? An undercover operator must be trained in the fundamentals of investigative work. He is first interviewed by our personnel department. He is given a polygraph examination to determine the truth of his statements and to discover the type of work he is best suited for. We also learn something about his personality, his character and his thinking in relation to undercover work.

When our polygraph examiner has given him a clean bill, he

is then referred to our undercover department where he is again interviewed. He is given oral and written tests to give us an idea of his capabilities, his ability to grasp a situation, his alertness to perceive dishonesty when it occurs or if it is in the forming stage. (Although I use the pronoun "he," we do use quite a few women in these jobs.)

The prospective undercover agent is fingerprinted, allowed to read reports from other agents to give him insight into the type of information desired.

Secrecy Is Vital

The art of placing an undercover agent in an organization is very important. The fewer people who know about it, the better.

The operators will go through regular channels of being hired, the same as any other employee. When they fill out applications, we make sure they can be checked out. In most instances, the operator will have previous experience in the line of work he is applying for, such as a stock clerk, shipping clerk, truck driver, forklift operator, inventory control expert, cashier, typist, chemical engineer, hotel manager, registered pharmacist, supermarket manager, and many other jobs.

Once the operator starts working, there may be an over-anxious executive wanting to know what is transpiring. Instead of consulting with the agency, he may try to talk to the operator while he or she is working. This is a sure way to break the cover of the operator, and our agents are trained never to tell anyone anything. All information is cleared through our headquarters and then relayed to the proper party.

We have meetings with our clients and counsel with them when we are ready to make any apprehensions. We discuss the matter with the client in full detail. Sometimes we interrogate on the information we have received from our operator; other times we will apprehend the employee in the act of stealing. The statements obtained are often for very large sums of money, and in many instances they involve more than one person. Restitution is usually sought, either from the bonding company or from the employee. Restitution, of course, is handled by management of the client company.

Background Screening and Employee Education

The business firm which conducts thorough background checks on all personnel before hiring, which gives extensive pre- and on-the-job training, will have a more efficient, honest and competent staff of workers than the firm that is negligent about these matters.

Employment rules and regulations must be followed through. Many of our clients have executives talk to groups of their managers and employees regarding rules and procedures. Employees are told what will happen to those involved in defalcations. They know of the great risks they will encounter should they succumb to temptation, the shame they will have to face with their families, the fact that they cannot be bonded again or get decent jobs.

Security heads and management must work together; they cannot let employees be tempted to commit acts of dishonesty. Employees must not have the opportunity to steal without fear. If an employee feels a company is not aware of what is going on and that nothing serious will happen if he gets caught, that is a signal for him to start stealing. Once he gets away with it, it mushrooms; not only does he start stealing big, but others in the organization do the same.

Importance of Security Controls

Twenty years ago employers were more interested in checking on the courtesy and efficiency of their clerks than in dishonesty. The situation is completely different today. Employers want to know who is stealing and how they are stealing. They are interested in knowing how to plug up the loopholes so they will not happen again.

Controls are the answer. Employee orientation must be complete. Security must be kept up to date. The security program should be reviewed frequently for timeliness and effectiveness. It should be part of every person's working day and should motivate the entire staff by incentives, bulletins and a full flow of information that makes every employee realize that security controls protect his bread and butter.

The use of outside agency security specialists, discreetly serving and protecting top management, is recommended. Professional help is valuable for special situations, just as surgeons are needed for operations. One can maintain good health by following sensible rules of proper diet, rest and exercise. However, when there is a dangerous illness or organic crisis, a specialist is needed to restore good health.

Top level management must be alert, informed and interested. Executive emphasis on security sets the tone for lower-echelon supervision and subordinate employees. Only by organized and efficient management action will losses be minimized, dishonesty reduced, and protection achieved. Controls are the cornerstones of profits.

Thomas Jefferson said, "Eternal vigilance is the price of liberty." We at Merit like to think eternal vigilance is the price of survival.

Nathan T. Glaser

Mr. Glaser is president of Merit Protective Service, Inc. of New York, leading shopping service, and vice-president of Globe Security Systems, Inc., the fourth largest guard service in the country.

A leading security analyst, Mr. Glaser has been with the Merit organization since they hired him as a boy, working in every phase of shopping service work, from wrapping "shopped goods," his first job, through supervision and interrogation, to the presidency.

Chapter 11

UNDERCOVER INVESTIGATION:
MANAGEMENT'S PERISCOPE

By Earl F. Lorence

During the last decade, employee theft has changed radically. No longer a one-man, do-it-yourself larceny, thievery—like many other fields today—has undergone a period of specialization. Too, rapid business growth has made it almost impossible for today's executive to see everything going on within his company. As one executive puts it, "Show me a company whose management knows everything that is happening in that company, and I'll show you a pretzel stand or some other one-man operation."

In addition, rapid expansion, often accompanied by high employee turnover, has led to carelessness in hiring, as well as inadequate hit-or-miss training programs. Added to this, too, is the age-old fact that employee performance while under observation by management is all too often a very unreliable index of employee behavior when management is occupied elsewhere.

The demand for a new approach to the problem of employee theft has given fresh impetus to an old security technique that had been relatively dormant for some years—undercover investigation.

As recently as five years ago, industrial and commercial firms

---

©1965, 1975, Security World Publishing Co., Inc.

and institutions were not too receptive to undercover investigation as a possible solution to their security problems. The word "undercover" in some quarters suggested a cloak-and-dagger approach incongruous to normal business affairs. But the stakes are higher and rising, and so are the losses. The executive who commented a few years ago, "You just don't go around spying on your own people," now wants an effective way to stop thefts and to protect those employees who have not yet succumbed to temptation. Especially within the last two years, there has been a marked change in management's attitude toward undercover investigation.

Purpose of Undercover Investigation

The role of commercial undercover investigation is essentially the same the world over, no matter what title it may be given. From the days when the topic was considered taboo in many quarters, undercover investigation has inherited such euphemistic labels as "management advisory service," "management engineering survey," and "management security control." The purpose, however, remains the same.

The purpose of undercover investigation is this: To gain for management skilled eyes and ears to observe employees on the job, under normal working conditions, without stirring up employee suspicion or resentment.

A good undercover operative can detect many irregularities which affect production and profits—e.g., theft of merchandise or cash, inventory shortages, kickbacks, padded expenditures, spying by competitors, time-card cheating, gambling or drinking on the job, poor or weak supervision, misuse of company materials, careless handling of merchandise, malingering, and practically everything else of concern to management.

In one case, production was inexplicably low on the night shift, so low that day supervision brought the problem to management. An undercover agent quickly brought them up-to-date. Employees had a system for time-card cheating whereby six employees would "disappear" each morning during the 4 a.m. lunch break. Their associates would punch their time cards at 8 a.m. Altogether about 15 employees shared in this practice, rotating the time off equally among themselves. Ironically, the actual production time among these employees during any four-hour period amounted to about

90 minutes, with the rest of the time spent in goldbricking, fooling around and drinking beer. Source of the trouble was a night foreman who was on the job but had become completely indifferent, with the result that the entire night shift operation had become a drain on the company, rather than supplementing productivity.

In another instance, the night supervisor at the pie plant turned out to be one of his company's strongest competitors. For a period of about nine months, he sold boxes of pies to employees and neighborhood residents for a fraction of the retail cost, pocketing the money. Those who bought pies from him (on the company's premises!) assumed the money was going to the company.

Employee Attitudes Source of Loss

Besides theft and dishonesty, the operative is in a good position to study employee attitudes and work habits, and can make recommendations for boosting morale, reducing turnover, increasing output, tightening security, etc., which can help management avert problems and correct troublespots.

One large soap plant had become a haven for employee thieves, loafers, time-card cheaters and other wrongdoers until undercover investigation helped management take corrective action. Two employees, for example, had a self-made room in the stock area where they took turns sleeping or reading obscene literature during working hours, often for as long as three hours at a stretch. A number of other employees used the roof of the plant to cache stolen merchandise, which they later removed from the premises by way of an adjoining building. Dice games and drinking on the job were common among many employees. The irregularities were so widespread throughout the plant that it took one undercover man posing as a porter three months to complete the investigation.

Storm Signals for Management

There are many symptoms or storm signals which indicate the need for undercover investigation. These are but a few of them:

- Inventory shortages
- "Mysterious" disappearance of merchandise or cash
- A drop in profits despite a boost in sales

- Excessive overtime
- Time-card cheating
- Excessive employee turnover
- A sharp drop in employee morale
- Unauthorized discounts
- Excessive employee damaging of merchandise
- Unreported shortages in merchandise from suppliers
- Frequent customer complaints.

Vendor complaints led to an investigation at a large store in upstate New York, where it was found that the shipping clerk who packed merchandise for return to suppliers was switching mailing labels on his way to the post office, pasting a label bearing his home address over the correct label.

When undercover work is performed by a professional security agency, the operative does not report his findings directly to the client, nor attempt to contact the client under any circumstances. Instead, he regularly makes oral and written reports to his supervising investigator or case control officer, who in turn sends written reports to the client, as well as making oral reports where immediate action is indicated.

Secrecy Vital

Reporting to the client is a prearranged procedure by which written reports as well as all bills are sent directly to the client's home under the name of a "cover" company. (Where billing is direct to the client's office, a "cover" name is also used.) Telephone reports to the client are never made through a company switchboard.

Apart from knowing the investigation is in process, the client in many cases does not know the identity of the operative, nor is the investigation itself a matter of general knowledge among company management. The security officer and one or two top officials of the firm very often are the only ones who know about the investigation. The personnel department is seldom told about it, for reasons I will bring out a little later, except in those instances where the personnel department has the security function. In fact, this investigation is conducted so carefully and confidentially that even where two operatives are assigned to the same location, neither one knows of the other's presence or identity.

That's merely another precaution against arousing suspicion among employees who might otherwise detect a mutual interest between two investigators; also, it helps avoid problems that could result if two investigators knew of each other's presence and each assumed the other was covering and reporting a specific irregularity. "I assumed you were taking care of that," management's chronic headache, has no place in a competent investigation.

Similarly, management's corrective steps against irregularities uncovered by the operative are taken in a way that will not reveal the operator's identity or anything else relating to the source of information. This is true both during and after the investigation.

How Is the Operative Placed?

The undercover operator must be skilled not only as an investigator, but also as the employee he is acting as, whether it be janitor or executive. The operative is on his own, except for his contact with his supervising investigator, and he is well aware that he can't walk around like Ian Fleming's Agent 007 and expect to win the confidence of fellow employees.

As an investigator, he (or she, since many undercover jobs require female operatives) has acute perception, a detailed knowledge of many subjects in business, and a good memory for names, dates and other facts. He is an extrovert, makes friends easily, and knows how to mix well with people at all levels of business activity, depending upon the assignment. But one of his most valuable assets is his ability to assume the role and character best suited to the assignment and the job for which he is ostensibly hired. He may have a master's degree in business administration, but if he's unloading a truck at a receiving platform it's not going to be visible.

Since the operative must join the client-company as a regular paid employee in order to conduct the covert investigation effectively, he first has to meet the company's hiring requirements without arousing suspicion among employees.

That's one of the reasons we feel personnel departments should not be alerted to the investigation—we have found from experience that anything that upsets the natural relationship between the client-company and the employee-operative can frustrate the investigation and delay results. In one case, for instance, the operative received such preferential treatment that it aborted his efforts as an investigator– not because he was suspected of being an investigator, but because his fellow employees were sure he was related to the bosses, so they didn't trust him!

Competence in Dual Role Required

Today the recruitment of qualified undercover operatives at the larger security agencies is no longer the problem it was some years ago when this form of investigation was fairly new. Applicants are drawn from practically every walk of life, with experience embracing all aspects of American enterprise. In most instances, the applicants have had prior investigative experience with one or more of a number of governmental, municipal or private security agencies.

In other instances, the applicant may have a good business background and a natural inclination toward undercover work, but little practical experience as an investigator. So long as the applicant has the aptitudes essential to this type of work—natural curiosity, good memory, extroverted personality, etc.—most larger agencies will consider hiring him in a trainee capacity. In that case he may spend the first few days doing nothing more than reading case histories and reports by other operatives. He may then work for several weeks on other types of investigations (surveillance, background, pre-employment, specific loss) before being assigned to his first undercover case.

It is interesting to note that most beginners in undercover work do as conscientious a job as their more experienced colleagues, for the simple reason that they do not yet trust their own judgment in evaluating the relative importance of any incident, so they report everything they see or hear.

The Right Place at the Right Time

For best results, the operative should be placed in a position where he can move about freely. For a general undercover investigation, the job of porter or janitor, for example, can be a real eye-opener to a good operative; the porter is able to canvass the building and explore corners and hide-aways inaccessible to the employee in a restrictive position. For a specific loss investigation, of course, the operative is placed within the department involved.

From the time the operative is hired by the client-company, he receives regular wages, based on the company's normal pay scale, so that company records do not reveal his dual role.

Charges for undercover work vary according to assignments. A typical charge to a client is about $200 per week per operative (in addition to the regular salary the operative earns for the job in which he is acting).

More so than any other form of industrial security, undercover work requires patience on the part of the client and the operative.

"Instant Success" Rare

The results are not always immediate. It usually takes even the best of operatives a couple of weeks to acclimate himself to the new job, to win the confidence of fellow employees, and to build the information sources essential to the investigation. But no matter how expert the operative may be, he's no miracle worker. Sometimes he gets or makes a couple of good breaks, and within a few days on the job he comes up with information the client never dreamed he'd uncover. Other times he may have to play the waiting game.

Although the biggest share of undercover work concerns the investigation of specific losses, there is a noticeable trend among many companies toward the use of general or preventive undercover investigation three or four times a year, rotating it among certain key departments.

How Is the Information Used?

Interrogation is an important adjunct to undercover work, and is usually conducted after the operative completes the fact-finding part of the investigation and terminates his employment with the client-company. In a number of cases, the polygraph is used during the interrogation to verify the truthfulness of the suspect's statements regarding collusion, the whereabouts of stolen merchandise, method of operation, and other pertinent information.

Although the decision of whether or not the company should prosecute dishonest employees is left to management, should the client decide to do so (and many firms do, these days), most security agencies will testify for the company in court or before a grand jury.

The willingness to fit the punishment to the crime is a fairly recent trend, and one which security and law enforcement people feel was a long time coming, especially where some of the firms now prosecuting had previously refused to prosecute under any circumstances. Without the threat of punishment, no system of protection can be effective. Until a few years ago, when a businessman had a dishonesty loss, he usually spoke of it in whispers—"nobody wants to hurt a man's reputation or his family," as if the person had not already done so! Instead of really solving the problem, management was allowing dishonest employees to move freely from one company to the next, giving the habitual thief new opportunities to use his talents.

Then, too, the lack of publicity lulled many firms into believing that this type of loss was rare. The fact is that employees are pilfering from American business and industry an estimated $2 billion a year, more than triple the rate of theft in the United States by all burglars, robbers and auto thieves combined.

How Widespread Is It?

Some years ago, the head of a giant plant engaged in government contract work wanted a publicity picture of the thousands of employees coming out of the main gates at quitting time. To set the scene, the gates were locked and camera men were stationed in the watchman's tower. The workmen, however, did not know what was planned. The scuttlebutt was that the F.B.I. was going to search them all for stolen parts and tools.

When the picture was snapped, the gates were opened and the workmen left for home. On the ground where they had been standing were over 4,000 items of tools, parts, scrap, soap, towels, and even a 15-pound sledge hammer—all left behind by a few thousand good, honest, hard-working people who had intended to take these articles without permission.

The Role of Security

How does security fit into the picture? What assurance does management have that a good, tight security program will *prevent* employee stealing?

None whatsoever, if the management is looking for *total* prevention!

On the other hand, there is much that planned security can do and is doing to help control losses and reduce pilferage and other irregularities to minimum levels.

Depending on the size of the company, number of employees, method of operation, etc., security needs for maximum control vary widely. One employer may find that a single uniformed guard is an adequate deterrent against irregularities; another may require several guards; a third may need guards, plus closed circuit television, and so on across the entire spectrum of security services— pre-employment screening, background and reference verification, pre-employment and specific loss polygraph testing, intrusion detection systems, surveillance, and of course undercover investigation.

The most important consideration for any company is that management must constantly view security in terms of its changing needs; the dishonest employee thrives best on management indifference and ignorance.

In short, while undercover investigation alone offers no panacea for the $2 billion headache ailing American business and industry, when integrated with a well-planned program for supervised honesty, modern professional security techniques can help employers discover weaknesses, plug the gaps, solve the "mysteries" and prevent the many losses that often occur for no other reason than laxness in security.

Earl F. Lorence

Mr. Lorence has been director of security for the Metropolitan Tobacco Company in Long Island City, N.Y., since 1967. Prior to that he served as chief of the investigation and polygraph divisions of Interstate Security Services, Inc., of New York City, one of the nation's largest professional agencies specializing in security services.

A former detective sergeant with the Erie County Sheriff's Department in Buffalo, Mr. Lorence has had more than twenty years' experience as an investigator and polygraph examiner. He holds a degree in police science from the Erie County Technical Institute, where he later taught. He has instructed classes in interrogation procedures at the Erie County Law Enforcement Training Academy.

A graduate of the Keeler Polygraph Institute in Chicago, Mr. Lorence is a member and past president of the Polygraph Examiners of New York State; a member of the Society of Professional Investigators; and a past president of the Police Science Alumni Association.

Chapter 12

THE USES OF AGENCY INVESTIGATION

By Henry C. Neville

Meeting the demands of modern business and industry has necessitated a major expansion of the investigations department of
Pinkerton's, Inc., and has brought about changes in operating methods that founder Allan Pinkerton and his associates never dreamed
about when the company opened its doors for business in 1850.

An appraisal of current investigations reveals that business and
industry are confronted with a large preponderance of bugging and
wiretapping offenses. A cross-section of the other current investigative cases reveals that clients range all the way from a jet engine
manufacturer to a women's apparel shop owner. Activities of investigators range from a shopping trip to determine whether a
client's products are being sold under Fair Trade prices to surveillance of a $40,000-a-year executive whose conduct in his off-hours
is considered by his employer as detrimental to the firm's image.

©1969, 1975, Security World Publishing Co., Inc.

Internal Theft

A large number of cases require investigations to solve theft and pilferage offenses committed against employers. A significant number of these cases involve collusion and require extensive undercover work to identify the offenders.

Internal surveys constitute another major investigative area. Cases include such diverse assignments as checking on the after-hours activities of a private luncheon club, trailing fuel oil trucks to observe drivers suspected of making oil deliveries to their homes and those of friends.

The Problem Employee

Many of the investigations conducted for business and industry come at the request of top officers, the majority from company presidents themselves. A number of these cases have concerned the problem employee—the man who has a record of loyal service but who for reasons not obvious is failing to meet his job responsibilities. Among such cases, it has been discovered that increased responsibilities may have caused pressures which the employee sought to escape in diversions like gambling and drinking.

Business and industry are giving high priority also to background investigations of key personnel being promoted or hired for executive and middle management positions. They are more wary about their choice of personnel for positions of trust and responsibility, and as a result are relying more heavily than ever before on investigative service organizations to evaluate and authenticate employee backgrounds before filling the vacancies.

The complexities of modern business make the job of the professional investigator considerably more difficult than his "frontier detective" predecessor. The "bad guys" don't all wear black hats or have their pictures posted on "wanted" circulars. Most of the offenders today are faceless and their names don't strike fear in the hearts of the townspeople. Unfortunately in too many cases, they *are* the townspeople—thousands of workers in plants and offices throughout the country. They fill positions at every level—from janitor and factory worker to corporation executive. Consequently, investigators must be selected with skills and talents that closely match those of people suspected of wrongdoing. The match-up gives them the advantage of an occupational identity with their adversaries, and their true roles as investigators remain secret.

To meet the wide variety of problems occasioned by the diverse nature of business and industry, Pinkerton's has developed a force of male and female investigators who collectively have at their command some two dozen languages and more than 100 different skills that can be applied at managerial, financial, clerical, technical, and journeyman levels. A large number of these personnel also have Defense Department clearance which permits them to conduct investigations at plants engaged in classified work for the government. Although the company's policy prevents its investigators from conducting any bugging or electronics eavesdropping, they are expertly trained in de-bugging operations to service clients who suspect incidents of industrial espionage.

Background Checks

The scope and variety of investigations continue to widen. An increasing number of cases require employee background checks. One client admitted that his company had at one time spent more time and money checking out an electric typewriter than it did to verify the background of a $20,000-a-year executive.

Recent Pinkerton's investigations for companies seeking managerial help have turned up some bizarre and unusual findings. A man who was being considered for the position of investment counsellor had a police record that not only showed that he was a shoplifter but that he conducted his escapades in female attire. The police report added that he wore cosmetics such as lipstick, false eyelashes, and eye make-up. Moreover, he was described by police "as a rather attractive large female."

In another investigation, an official of the client firm was considering two individuals for positions of trust in the company. It was learned that one of the prospects had been indicted for business fraud in the amount of $66,000.

A man applying for an opening as cost and budget specialist for a major manufacturer proved unsuitable when the investigation revealed that his previous employer fired him for his uncooperative attitude toward fellow employees and his failure to maintain accurate records. The investigation also disclosed that this same individual proved inadequate in a prior position when his employer revealed that the man took ten weeks to perform an inventory count, whereas his predecessor accomplished the same task in three weeks. The employer said "the man was hired initially because he cited previous inventory experience on his application. His performance indicated he had no knowledge along these lines."

A check on the qualifications of another applicant for a managerial post revealed that the man was actively engaged in the American Nazi party. His application, however, indicated no such affiliation.

These cases typify a ground swell developing among employers who express their "right to know" about applicant backgrounds simply to safeguard their companies' reputations and their investments in plants, property, products, and equipment.

Techniques of Investigation

There are many aids to effective investigation. These include the motion picture camera, the polygraph, handwriting analysis, surveillance, and the ingredient of "dogged perseverance," which applies when there are no clues or those which lead the investigator up blind alleys.

On a recent case for a large mail-order house serving the U.S. and Canada, the solution to a $150,000 theft of watches, TV and hi-fi sets, rifles, stereos and transistor radios came about because the investigators just wouldn't give up despite the absence of fingerprints or other tangible clues.

The initial investigation revealed that the stolen merchandise was transported from the company's warehouse in one of its own vehicles. A number of burglar alarms and other security devices were bypassed when the thieves ransacked the warehouse. The facts strongly suggested that the theft was the work of professionals who undoubtedly had "inside information" concerning the plant layout and its security equipment.

When the stolen vehicle was located, it was devoid of any fingerprints or other clues to trace the identity of the thieves or the whereabouts of the merchandise.

Several days later, two men were arrested by the police while attempting to burglarize a nearby plant. One man was wearing an expensive wristwatch which subsequently was identified as an item from the list of missing merchandise. However, the lead reached a dead end when the men were advised of their rights and each refused to make any statement concerning the stolen watch.

In the meantime, our investigators had been checking into background information of the insured's employees. As a result, several were singled out for questioning and they subsequently admitted that many employees engaged in stealing merchandise from the warehouse. The interrogation also produced a lead that a former employee was possibly responsible for the theft in question.

Almost simultaneously, the police came into possession of a blueprint of the plant. Detailed handwritten notes on the blueprint disclosed exact locations in the warehouse where expensive merchandise was stored. It further pinpointed the locations of security devices and alarms covering vehicle, storage, and other vulnerable access areas.

Our investigators then secured all past and present employment applications for the purpose of comparing each individual's handwriting with that on the blueprint. One man's handwriting matched—the former employee who had been singled out previously as the likely suspect.

When the handwriting analysis was given to police authorities, a warrant was issued for the man's arrest. He was taken into custody and upon questioning disclosed that he had sold the blueprint and a set of warehouse keys to the two burglars previously mentioned. Still another man was implicated, and after his arrest, more than $50,000 in stolen mail order merchandise was recovered from his home.

An additional $20,000 in appliances stolen from other establishments was also recovered and returned to stores in several nearby communities.

A police check of the individual caught with the merchandise in his home revealed that he had a record for burglary and for dealing in stolen goods.

The four men involved in the operation are under grand jury indictment and are presently awaiting trial. Cost of the investigation amounted to less than $1,000.

Increased Use of Private Investigators

The trend toward increased use of private investigators by both insurance companies and private industry is continuing. To meet the demand for services, a larger pool of experienced supervisors has been organized and more intensive training for investigators has already been initiated.

Personnel Research Service

Because many clients are now requiring more extensive background information about their job candidates, Pinkerton's has already instituted a personnel research service as an outgrowth of its investigations department. Investigations are either undertaken on a "per lead" basis—checking background information which the employer cannot verify himself—or compiling a complete file of the individual applicant's qualifications. Investigators are trained to cover two important aspects in the full-scale operation:

1. The routine check which shows a candidate to be honest, stable and hardworking, along with verification of his educational background and moral character.

2. An "in-depth" report giving the employer an insight into the applicant's qualifications including:

- Scope of previous responsibilities.
- Willingness to accept difficult job assignments.
- Ability to make correct decisions when confronted with important deadlines.
- Awareness of and conformity to the economics affecting any given operation.
- Cooperation with fellow employees—superiors and subordinates—when the workload becomes excessive.
- Ability to organize and resolve complex problems.
- Attention devoted to small but important details.
- Judgment exercised in delegating work to others.
- Poise, confidence, and leadership qualities displayed in the presence of company associates, vendors, suppliers, distributors and representatives of outside business and industrial firms.

Under no circumstances does the investigator attempt to draw a conclusion from these interviews. Information relative to the foregoing points is given to the prospective employer in concise, narrative form, and the final decision rests with him. But, the factual material establishes a convincing pattern of "what makes the man tick." It furnishes the collective viewpoints of past employers and offers a solid basis for determining whether the applicant is what he represents himself to be.

Henry C. Neville

As vice president of investigations for Pinkerton's, Inc., Henry C. Neville supervises investigations handled by the firm's 106 offices in the U.S. and Canada. Before his appointment to this position in 1970, he was assistant to the president, and was responsible for developing and implementing special services and security products.

Mr. Neville joined Pinkerton's New York office in 1956 as an investigator. In 1960 he was appointed to the Department of Investigation in New York. He is the author of Pinkerton's basic training manual for investigators. He was named assistant vice president and manager of the firm's Eastern region in 1968.

A graduate of Hofstra University, Mr. Neville is a member of the New York State Association of Chiefs of Police, the International Association for Identification, and the National Sheriffs Association.

V.
INTERROGATIONS
AND
CONFESSIONS

Chapter 13

AN INTRODUCTION TO INTERROGATION

By Warren E. King

The art of interrogation is an asset of great value to the security officer; yet proficiency in this art often falls short of desired standards. Much of the security officer's time is devoted to questioning people, and success or failure usually results in direct ratio to the investigator's ability to obtain the truth.

This is the purpose of interrogation: to determine truth. The methods vary, but the basic ingredients are common to all: objectivity, integrity, insight, experience in human relationships, understanding of cause-effect relationships, salesmanship, patience, tact, empathy, ability to establish rapport, logical mind, perception, perseverance, motivation and alertness.

Of course, "spontaneous" confessions are quite common. However, a confession obtained without consideration for truth is as worthless as a decision made without due regard for facts. Neither is valid.

Other important factors are: Proper investigation of background concerning the material under consideration and the subject to be

© 1964 by Warren King. Reprinted by permission.

interrogated; location of interrogation, timing, duration, planning and number of persons present.

Theodore Reik, in his book *The Compulsion to Confess*, stated the phenomenon of confession is, in terms of the subconscious, an overpowering guilt feeling and desire for punishment. . . "There is . . . an impulse growing more and more intense, suddenly to cry out his secret in the street before all people, or in milder cases, to confide in at least one person, to free himself from the terrible burden. The work of confession is, thus, that emotional process in which the social and psychological significance of the crime becomes preconscious and in which all powers that resist the compulsion to confess are conquered."[4]

In this we see the motivation for confession. With guilty subjects, in truth there will be confession. Unlike "third degree" methods, the scientific approach precludes inconsistencies and deception.

The role of the interrogator should aptly be likened to that of a salesman. "Truth Merchants" are selling a product much as the person who peddles wares. A "sale" will only evoke facts which are pure. We, therefore, see there is a definite method involved, not merely random conversation. The method applied will depend on the subject (not the case) and we recognize that each of us differs in many ways.

Acknowledging this fact, one may yet adopt specific "methods" with a wide variety of persons and achieve the end result. How then may we select a "proper method"? First, we *observe, identify and classify* our subject. Is he emotional or non-emotional? Nervous or calm? Strong or weak? Extroverted or introverted, etc.? After having completed this process through careful inquiry and observation, select a "method" which you have previously used with success when dealing with similar personalities. In this connection, a discipline in forensic psychology is desirable. In order to make value judgments of persons not well known to you, an innate ability to equate environment, training, social habits, motivation, somatic types and physiological factors is essential. You can then make a tentative hypothesis of your subject and apply either an emotional or logical approach.

---

[4] Theodore Reik, THE COMPULSION TO CONFESS. (New York: Farrar, Straus and Cudahy, 1945).

The Art of Interrogation

An effort will be made in this chapter to describe some of the "tools" of the interrogator, and to describe the methods by which they can be used most effectively. A study of the methods of interviewing and interrogating will familiarize the investigator with the basic principles of questioning, but *skill* can only be attained through the application of these principles in actual practice and self-analysis of the application.

Purpose and Importance

We must talk to a person or people to gather information, to assemble evidence, to prove or disprove the innocence or guilt of suspects, and many other things to get the complete picture of the incident. Interviews are staged when questioning witnesses, victims, and possible suspects. When the available evidence indicates the guilt of a suspect, we employ interrogation techniques in order to obtain a confession, admission, or other facts which may be used to further establish guilt or innocence.

It has been suggested, and probably correctly, that the reason so many unsolved crimes clutter up police records today is that someone, somewhere along the line, failed to properly interview or interrogate a witness or suspect. In so doing they failed to obtain important information which would have led to the guilty party and provided a basis for his or her prosecution. Many thousands of criminals are still free today after having successfully committed a crime, not because of their skill in evading detection, but because the police investigating the offense failed to ask the right question at the right time.

Despite adequate training and years of experience, some investigators never really excel in interrogation techniques. The reasons for this are many and include such factors as personality, physical factors, intelligence, prejudices, and others. An investigator can do much to improve himself along these lines if he really wants to. Self analysis is the first step. After determining his weakness he must then make a very determined effort to correct his deficiency and make a dynamic resolution never to fall into the old rut again.

In emphasizing the importance of interrogation, it must be remembered that it still is only a link in the chain of evidence which must be collected to form the basis of a case which will lead to criminal prosecution. If the interrogator could be trained as well as the scientist in the crime lab, the results in increased percentages of admissions and confessions might prove to be startling. It has been said before, and will be repeated again here, that probably in a large percentage of cases the *weakest* link in the chain of evidence is the interrogation. If ill-timed or inadequate interrogation doesn't destroy a case altogether it will, many times, cause a large number of additional unnecessary man-hours to be consumed during the investigation.

Qualifications for a Questioner

Anyone who has been active in security or law enforcement for any period of time has probably come in contact with another officer who seemed to excel in talking to suspects and getting them to tell their respective stories. These officers were able to extract admissions and confessions from suspects under the most adverse conditions while dealing with the most difficult personalities. How were they able to do this? What special talents or abilities did they have?

These special abilities are very subjective and we can only speak in generalities when we try to describe them. We can give a basic list of personality traits which would tend to give the interrogator the tools he needs to accomplish his mission. How he utilizes his tools will make the difference between a good and a poor questioner. A person can have all the ability he would ever need, yet it is quite useless unless he applies it in an effective manner.

A partial list of qualifications for a questioner might include the following.

Better-Than-Average Intelligence

Let us face this issue squarely. We are dealing with other human beings in our interrogation. They have the same opportunity to think as we do. Any advantage that we might gain over a suspect in the battle of wits is very important. One of the primary principles taught in military strategy is to never underestimate your opponent. This principle apparently was learned the hard way. We can certainly apply it in our dealings with people. To assume an offender is stupid and conduct the interrogation accordingly may be just what he wants you to do. Playing dumb is an old trick frequently used by criminals as an effective countermeasure during an interrogation.

The interrogator must consider the intellect of the suspect in planning his interrogation. He certainly couldn't use the same words and phraseology with a college professor that he would with a person with low intelligence. Here again the questioner must have the mental capacity to talk intelligently with either type of suspect on his particular level of understanding. Slang and semiobscene words might be quite necessary with the moron but would be completely out of place when talking to Joe College.

The interrogator should possess a proportionate amount of theoretical knowledge, usually gained through formal education, and practical knowledge, sometimes called common sense, learned mostly through experience and personal contacts. This "native" intelligence, as it is sometimes called, enables the questioner to gain information readily and easily while talking to a person. He doesn't have to write down everything he hears but can remember the basic trend of the conversation and record it later. He can evaluate the information quickly, retaining the relevant, valid, and reliable, discarding the irrelevant, invalid, and unreliable.

He can weigh possible angles of attack in the interrogation quickly, considering the mentality of the suspect, the general situation, the timing, the other factors. After selecting the angle of attack, he proceeds into the interrogation much better equipped than he would have been otherwise.

Perseverance

Many sessions of interrogations have been terminated by the interrogator just seconds away from a full confession. If we just knew *how many*, it might take some time to count the red faces among interrogators. Many times you can sense a break coming in the suspect and can proceed accordingly. Probably just as many times the break comes unexpectedly and sometimes even catches the interrogator off guard. It is impossible to read a person's mind and know just what is transpiring there during an interrogation. You very seldom know just what line of reasoning the suspect is using, even though we try to provide one during the questioning.

It has been this writer's experience to interrogate a subject for a long period of time and practically exhaust every possibility of reasoning in trying to reach the subject and convince him he should tell the truth. Then, after mentally giving up and starting out of the room, I was called back and confronted with a full confession by the suspect. The suspect finally had gotten some of the line of logic through his head and realized that his best possible course was to tell the truth and hope for the best. Probably just as many suspects have not called me back and would have come through with an admission or confession if I had interrogated for just another *five minutes more.*

Alertness

The questioner must be mentally alert at all times when talking to a suspect. Any slip of the tongue or revelation of any kind by the suspect that he knows more than he has been telling should be immediately seized upon by the interrogator and used to an advantage. Any physical irregularity such as excessive perspiration, inability to look the interrogator in the eye, excessive nervousness, enlarged pupils, dry mouth, flushed face, or slurred speech should be noted by the interrogator. These changes are characteristic of a person who is undergoing great emotional stress. These physiological changes are brought about by overactivity of the sympathetic branch of the autonomic nervous system. Usually they are indicative of guilty knowledge of some type, as often shown in lie detector examinations.

The interrogator must be several steps ahead of the suspect in his interrogation and should lead him, step by step, to the point where he is mentally ready to tell the truth. Several barriers may be encountered along this path of mental conditioning; however, the alert questioner will be ready for them and will shift his tactics accordingly.

Experience in Human Relations

This is, perhaps, the key with which a successful interrogator is able to unlock most doors. Experience with many types of personalities is the "best tool" of the security or law enforcement officer.

Man is a social animal. He has appetites for such biological needs as warmth, shelter, and food. What makes him *human?* Among other things, his ability to reason, to learn and retain knowledgeable data. As a social animal, he must learn to satisfy his needs in an environment with other humans.

In this connection, he must obtain his needs in a socially acceptable manner. When he is hungry, he obtains food. To steal food (and thus fulfill the biological need) is socially unacceptable—and may create a psychological need!

Similarly, man has a psychological need for security, recognition, love, and attention. These, too, he must obtain in a socially acceptable manner. When he feels insecure, he must be assured there are those who care.

The fact that he may be secure is immaterial. If he *thinks* he has a problem, the problem does exist, and must be resolved (actually or psychologically).

With this over-simplified introduction, let us inventory our personal experiences with others. How much or little do we know about people—their desires, needs, goals, demands, motivations, fears, loves and hates?

One shoplifter or clerk may commit theft to satisfy a biological need; another for attention or security. What motivates a person to engage in anti-social behavior? Sociologists have been seeking the answer for centuries.

There are many logical reasons for anti-social behavior, and many seemingly illogical ones, which we cannot, as yet, identify. All these factors relate to man's *individuality*. Because man is a product of his environment, with certain biological and psychological limitations and needs, we must try to meet him in his individual environment, and interrogate him along lines meaningful to him. We must have experience in human relations.

Objectivity

Keep an "open mind"! How frequently do investigators violate this important rule? We mentioned earlier the goal of interrogation is truth. The successful, competent interrogation must be conducted objectively, or it is relegated to "getting a cop-out."

Objectivity does not preclude the evaluation of preliminary information. The important difference is, no decision can be reached until all the evidence is adduced and evaluated. The interrogator must passionately avoid making "value judgments" based solely on the preliminary investigation.

Sometimes investigators, after reaching a hypothesis in the early stages of interrogation, cling to it unduly. The early position may be supported only by premature conclusions, yet they will continue to be influenced by it. The investigation is thus subordinated to a defensive battle. Objectivity should be the byword in all interrogations.

Understanding Cause-Effect Relationships

We must seek out the answer to why people act or react in a given manner. This is especially important to an interrogation. More than this, we must understand that individuals are motivated differently. Two persons may be exposed to a similar situation. One reacts in a socially accepted manner; the other in an anti-social way.

For example, Joe, a long-time employee, is familiar with routine procedures. He knows the vendors well; he may even know their habits and weaknesses. In this relationship, he may permit "padding of bills" for an under-the-table remuneration.

Sam, also a long-time employee, has been asked to fill in when Joe is absent. He is confronted with a padded bill. Depending on his particular feelings, he has two basic choices: Report the matter to his superiors (i.e., protect the vendor's criminal attempt), or overlook the matter, and in so doing, become involved in the criminal design.

What Sam does will depend on three things: 1) his basic integrity, 2) his feelings toward his employer, and 3) his feelings toward Joe. Any one of these factors could motivate him toward socially accepted or anti-social action.

You say: What does all this have to do with interrogation? My answer is: Until you have an understanding of cause-effect relationships, it is difficult, if not impossible, to provide a rationalization to the subject of your interrogation (suspect), and thereby provide a means of "saving face."

Integrity

This should be your most outstanding trait. To arrive at truth, the interrogator himself must be honest, sincere, fair, undividedly upright, truthful and free from deceit. Of all the basic tenets for successful interrogation, integrity is the most significant. You might be stripped of your material wealth, your loved ones, your home and country, but no one can take away your most precious possession. Develop it, maintain it, defend it. It will never fail you. Only you can control, keep, or lose your integrity.

Insight

When one has had experience in human relations, an understanding of cause-effect relationships, intelligence, logical mind, alertness and perception, along with objectivity, he has insight. Insight is the ability to look clearly below the surface—deeply below—to recognize and understand human behavior.

Empathy

This is the ability to put oneself in another's place (i.e., to understand another person; his feelings and reasons for being in his present circumstance). Empathy does not mean to sympathize. When you sympathize, the other person has a crutch on which to lean. Not so with empathy. When you use an empathetic approach, your subject feels that you are his friend because you understand *why* he is faced with a given problem.

Motivation

Experience has shown that a person who is properly motivated will do better than one who is not. Motivation (properly directed) can enable one to surpass many otherwise seemingly impossible situations. It is important to be highly motivated during the interrogation process. Your goal is truth. It can be attained. Along the way you may set up related "sub-goals" to prevent lack of the perseverance that is so important in any successful interrogation.

For example, your first objective is rapport. When your subject thinks he likes you, a line of conversation will develop. This will enable you (again, if properly directed) to determine his "truth-telling style." When this is achieved, relevant questions may be interjected to evaluate their effect on your subject.

By maneuvering your subject carefully, it will soon become apparent what line of reasoning the subject utilizes. Certain basic traits and/or rationalizations will be evoked; certain fears exposed. At the proper moment (timing), you will achieve your major goal—truth. To reach this goal, it's imperative you be properly motivated.

Tact

The dictionary defines this word as "a keen sense of how to deal with people and difficult situations *without giving offense;* the ability to say and do the right things; delicacy; diplomacy." One cannot overemphasize the importance of not saying or doing anything (unless planned) which would give offense to the subject. There is no place for prejudice or bias in any interrogation. This does not preclude the use of sympathetic awareness to a given situation. The interrogator might well utilize a subject's minority relationship to develop a rationalization for misdeeds. The important point to remember is: Your subject is keenly aware of you and what you say. Any indication of insincerity will be discerned readily. You must, above all else, be tactful.

Perception and Patience

One may perceive without having insight, but may not have insight without perception. This is an important distinction. Perception connotes the act of *observing* certain facts. Insight is the act of *understanding* these facts.

Patience is self-explanatory. Patience is a virtue; in interrogation, it is a *must.*

Logical Mind

The mass of information which necessarily precedes any successful interrogation requires a logical mind to assimilate and evaluate its importance. The who, what, when, why and how must be determined. Some of these questions remain unanswered and the interrogator, with a logical mind, must determine which areas need further clarification, and what must be ascertained. In addition, he must determine the relative importance of certain facts to avoid wasting unnecessary time on extraneous issues.

After reviewing the case and the subject's background, he must interview the investigators to verify and accumulate data. During interrogation, the exercise of a particular plan requires intensive concentration and implementation along logical lines. Certain factors must be weighed in the light of truth. The most effective means of classifying and evaluating such factors is a logical mind.

Ability to Establish Rapport

When one meets a stranger, frequently it is difficult to carry on a conversation. Once a feeling of mutual trust and understanding is developed, barriers (psychological protections) are removed, and one drops his guard.

The establishment of rapport is one of the more important prerequisites of successful interrogation. What one does or says is most important.

For example, if upon meeting your subject you indicate your displeasure by a gruff "good morning," a cool atmosphere results. Contrast this with the warm approach; a simple offer of a handshake, together with a smile and a friendly "Hello, how are you?" Such an approach will more readily develop and maintain mutual confidence. Successful interrogation demands mutual confidence. This does not prevent the application of certain psychological techniques, but does require care in their application. While dealing with many subjects requires ability in varied techniques, a basic requirement of any interrogation is conversation.

Conversation is an exchange of thoughts. In the interrogation process, these are not random remarks. Your planned approach directs the course of the exchange; but your ability to establish communication will develop rapport.

Salesmanship

Your product is truth. In order to be a good salesman, you should know your product well. When all else fails, come forward with an explanation of truth. Bushnell once said: "There is no fit search after truth which does not, first of all, begin to live the truth which it knows." Or Emerson's: "The greatest homage we can pay to truth is to use it."

Truth, in the final analysis, must conform with the facts. The good interrogator knows his product well; he lives it, he practices it, he projects it.

There are many other desirable qualities needed in a successful interrogator which have not been mentioned here. However, this partial list will give some idea of the particular abilities required for success. He must be able to apply these abilities, and no amount of discussion can substitute for actual experience.

Warren E. King

Warren King served with the Burbank (California) Police Department for fourteen years, reaching the rank of Lieutenant in 1968. A specialist in polygraph examinations and interrogation, Mr. King was a charter member of the California Association of Polygraph Examiners. He has taught Interrogation and Polygraph Methods at Long Beach State College.

In 1969 Mr. King left the police department to become a security consultant for a retail grocery chain in Southern California. Two years later, he moved to Northern California, where he is self-employed and does polygraph consulting work for the sheriff's departments in Shasta and Trinity Counties.

Chapter 14

INTERROGATION—
THE GUILTY REVEAL THEMSELVES

By Warren Holmes

From my experience administering thousands of polygraph examinations and conducting thousands of criminal interrogations, I would like to take you through a day in the life of "Harry Brown" —indulging, if you please, in a little imagination.

You have met Harry Brown a hundred times. He is a typical airline clerk employed in a major airlines office. Generally, he is 35 to 45 years of age, married, and has two children. He has been employed by the airline for seven years. He has a good record. Not a single complaint has ever been made against him which would necessitate an inquiry by the security department.

In the last year, however, the routine life of Harry Brown has undergone a severe change. Because of illness in his family he has become financially encumbered to the desperation point. To Harry Brown, the anguish of his personal problems is unbearable. This change in the life of Harry Brown has a direct bearing on his future relationship with you. For the first time he becomes a definite security risk.

© 1964, 1975, Security World Publishing Co., Inc.

Opportunity Arises

One morning he arrives at work and notices a deposit bag lying on a desk. He realizes immediately that the night clerk had forgotten to deposit this bag in the night vault. He knows from previous experience that there must be at least $2,000 to $3,000 in this bag. In those few moments an impulsive idea enters the mind of Harry Brown. The money in that bag is a solution to his personal financial problems. Varying thoughts race through his mind.

Unfortunately for Harry Brown, he is placed in the position which is the common denominator to all crime; the opportunity to steal and the belief that one's crime will go undetected. At this moment Harry Brown is consumed by need. This ready-made solution which lies before him is so enticing that it overcomes any personal fears he might have for the social reprisals of his act.

His conscience or his built-in braking system which has kept him honest all his life now slips, and he reaches out to steal the bag. He secretes the bag in a place where it will not be found, so that he might recover it later. From these moments on, Harry Brown is no longer the same human being. His entire behavior becomes a manifestation of his guilt.

Behavior Patterns

This brings me to the major point of my discussion. The study of human behavior associated with guilt feelings affords us the greatest opportunity to solve crimes. The thousands of individuals that I have seen parade through my office at the Miami Police Department attest to this fact. Too often we are without concrete evidence to substantiate guilt. In most instances we do not have any evidence to pinpoint the guilty party. It then becomes a question of an astute appraisal of each suspect's behavior in an effort to detect those signs which indicate guilt.

When you have interviewed thousands of individuals who have committed a wrongdoing and are possessed of guilt feelings, you become keenly aware that guilt definitely manifests itself in human behavior. You need not be a psychiatrist or a psychologist to observe this. The average investigator with years of experience develops an intuition and insight for perceiving guilt. These same investigators would have difficulty putting into words the basis for their success in perceiving guilt. This inability by no means negates the validity of their opinion.

Method Is Scientific

It is my contention that the observation of human behavior as it is associated with guilt feelings is not unscientific but based upon sound psychological principles. After you have conducted thousands of criminal interrogations it becomes apparent that the guilty reveal themselves through definite common behavioral patterns. It is my intention to help you read these patterns. To do this, let us return to our imaginary subject, Harry Brown.

After the commission of his crime, Harry Brown becomes enveloped by the emotions of fear and guilt. The counterpart to the mental experience of an emotion is a physiological feeling. The emotions of fear and guilt express themselves in extremely unpleasant sensations. Technically, these unpleasant sensations or feelings are called stress. Prolonged stress can take its toll upon human beings.

Harry Brown, now possessed of fear and guilt, becomes a victim of this terrible stress, but like all human beings, he possesses a psychological phenomenon to cope with stress. This psychological phenomenon consists of coping or defense mechanisms. There are many types of defense mechanisms and we employ them in different ways to handle stress. Human beings will not always use the same defense mechanisms in coping with stress arising out of fear and guilt feelings, but they will use one of them. Recognizing and understanding defense mechanisms affords us the best opportunities to perceive guilt in human beings.

Defense Mechanisms

In the Lie Detection Bureau of the Miami Police Department we made an extensive study of recognizing defense mechanisms associated with guilt. Our experience proved that we could many times pick out the guilty party by his employment of certain defense mechanisms. Naturally we had to be careful that these defense mechanisms were not being used to cope with guilt not associated with the crime in question. We were not right 100 percent of the time, but our knowledge of defense mechanisms was the greatest aid we had in picking out the guilty party.

During your interrogation of Harry Brown you might see him employ several different types of defense mechanisms. At this point I would like to discuss those defense mechanisms that are generally used by guilty subjects.

All of the defense mechanisms express themselves in the verbalizations of the subject and his over-all demeanor. Harry Brown might employ the defense mechanism of disassociation. If so, he would appear to be there in the interrogation room in body but not in mind. He has disassociated himself from his act by a kind of "thinking away" process.

In this case, Harry Brown would lack animation during the discussion. His responses would be vague and extremely evasive. He would make an effort to talk about anything but the crime in question. He will describe in great detail an incident or situation having nothing to do with the crime in question. When questioned specifically about the crime itself, his answers will be in general terms and very abrupt. He will tell you that he has not thought about the crime. He does not suspect anyone and has no idea how the crime was committed.

Appears Preoccupied

During a pause in the interrogation you will notice that this subject has a distant look in his eye and a vacant expression. He appears to be preoccupied. He lacks a desire to enter into the spirit of the conversation. He becomes animated in his discussion only at those times when the discussion is concerning something other than the crime in question. At times this subject gives the impression that the utterance of each word is a great effort. To this subject his act is intolerable. Being forced to recall it and to defend himself by deception requires great exertion on his part.

This subject will not take the initiative at any time during the conversation. He will not volunteer any information and will tell you in essence that he has been too busy to give any thought as to who might have stolen the missing deposit bag. This generally is your best clue.

Experience has told us that the average individual is an armchair detective. He actually loves to discuss his thoughts on how the crime might have been committed. The subject who tells you that he has not given any thought to the crime nor does he suspect anyone, in most instances is practicing deception. This individual in actuality does not have to think about the crime; he already knows the answer.

Practices Evasion

Frequently during your conversation with the subject he will use the expressions "not that I recall," and "to the best of my knowledge." This subject practices evasion to the nth degree. He refuses to be pinpointed by "yes" and "no" answers. When you ask him to describe his activities on or about the time of the crime, he will be extremely vague, yet he will describe in great detail his activities during times not associated with the crime. He will make an effort to use up time by answering questions at great length that are not injurious to him. You will catch him frequently ending sentences abruptly and then becoming very sullen and staring into space for long periods of time. He will not reactivate the conversation unless you do so.

In a controlled situation, where one is fearful of being detected in his lies, it takes a great deal of mental energy to practice deception. This subject wants to "think away" from the crime. He does not want to be forced back to the act of lying to defend himself. This subject many times gives the impression of being physically exhausted. The amount of energy that he has exerted to defend himself and to hide his guilt has taken its toll. The defense mechanism of disassociation as it is revealed in criminal interrogation is best described by one word, evasiveness.

Projection

Our imaginary subject, Harry Brown, also may employ the defense mechanism of projection. Those who employ this particular defense mechanism demonstrate a great deal of hostility toward the investigator and everyone in general. They project their guilt. They displace outwardly all that becomes troublesome from within. It is an externalization of an internal menace.

This subject will blame everyone else for his problems but himself. He will not accept guilt but will thrust it upon others. He pretends to be highly indignant about being questioned. Knowing full well that he is the guilty party, he will blame the police, his employer or anyone else he can think of for the fact that the crime is committed. It is important to understand that his display of hostility is a defense for his guilt. In other words he attempts to take the offensive during the interrogation period by this display of hostility which affords him the best defense. He pretends to become highly incensed when you even insinuate that he could be the guilty party.

Actually a subject who employs the defense mechanism of projection is "running scared." Once you have obtained a confession from this type of subject it is interesting to note how docile he becomes. It is quite apparent at this time that this projection of hostility toward others was nothing more than a defense mechanism. In most instances this subject in reality is angry with himself. He is angry that he committed a crime and he is angry over the possibility of being found out. This anger he projects upon others. In essence, his whole demeanor seems to scream out, "How dare you interrogate me concerning this crime?"

In conjunction with the two defense mechanisms of disassociation and projection, one frequently sees a third defense mechanism called rationalization. It is important to realize that defense mechanisms can be employed by themselves or in conjunction with others. If Harry Brown were to employ the defense mechanism of rationalization he would give many "good" reasons for his behavior rather than the real reasons. He probably would state that the missing deposit bag was lost and that he did not believe it to be stolen. In the next breath he would point out—what difference does it make, anyway, the airline has a lot of money and it will never miss two or three thousand dollars. He will go on to relate that the poor fellow who may have stolen the money probably was underpaid and therefore what he did really was not stealing.

Minimizes Crime

Of course, if a subject talks in this vein, in most instances, he really is talking about himself. He constantly minimizes the nature of the crime. When you ask this subject if he suspects anybody, he immediately points out that everyone employed by the airline is basically good. In his opinion, no one would deliberately steal the money. The guilty party who employs the defense mechanism of rationalization has thoroughly convinced himself that he was justified in his act. Even prior to a possible confession, everything this subject states will be of an excuse-making nature.

"Good Guy" Pose

Harry Brown also may use the defense mechanism of identification. This subject is the image maker. He portrays himself as holier-than-thou. This is someone who would lead you to believe he has never even had an off-color thought. To hear him tell it, he is as pure as the driven snow. He begins the conversation by telling you what a nice guy he is, how honest he is, how many times he goes to church, how he never would commit a wrong.

He constantly attempts to ingratiate himself with his interrogator. He identifies himself with all of those things that are considered good in our environment. He carries this to such an extreme that it is obvious he is employing the defense mechanism of identification.

There are many other defense mechanisms which you see demonstrated each day during an interrogation session. Space does not permit outlining all. My purpose will be accomplished if you will develop a further interest in the study of defense mechanisms as clues to possible guilt.

Guilt Consumes Subject

Now let me reiterate what I said in the beginning. Guilt and fear consume a guilty subject. Everything he does or says is a manifestation of that guilt. The signs are there for you to read. You can formalize this ability to achieve even greater success in the detection of guilt. Make an objective study of the behavior of those individuals you interrogate. Make notes on those statements which seem to emanate from the use of defense mechanisms. If you are fortunate enough to have obtained a confession, go over your notes. You will be amazed how revealing these statements were, despite the fact that they preceded a confession and the assurance of guilt.

You will discover that with the guilty subject all of his remarks preceding his confession had a logical basis and that they were in defense of the "self." You will state to yourself, "My God, in so many words he was telling me he was guilty all the time."

You will discover that no remarks are made by chance. Sigmund Freud pointed this out a long time ago. Freud contended that, if he asked a human being to suddenly mention a four-digit number, he could actually prove that the number given was not accidental but based upon an association with numbers significant to the individual, such as a phone number, house number, etc.

Remarks Significant

During an interrogation, if a subject suddenly blurts out a statement not in context with what you are talking about, there is a definite psychological basis for this remark. In most instances this out-of-context remark will have a direct association with the subject's guilt.

For example, if the subject suddenly exclaimed, "Boy, these hospitals get away with murder with the rates they charge," it is quite possible that, after obtaining a confession, you will find out that your subject has a tremendous hospital bill to pay and the pressure of this bill was the motivating factor behind his stealing the missing deposit bag. Harry Brown will reveal his guilt if you are astute enough to listen between his words.

At this point I would like to digress a bit and discuss the human practice of telling untruths. Never underestimate the capacity of human beings to lie. Contrary to what people might think, lying is not foreign to the nature of human beings. The act of lying to others as well as to oneself is necessary sometimes to maintain stability of mind. Many thoughts are too intolerable or too traumatic for the human mind to accept. In this respect, we play mental gymnastics with ourselves.

Lying Is "Natural"

There seems to be a predisposition in our nature which facilitates the act of telling a lie. It begins at a very early age. The fantasy thinking of a child is playful self-deception. As we grow older, self-deception becomes so integrated in our personality structure that it is done automatically on the unconscious level. It is important to understand that the basis of all lying is in defense of the "self," in that we lie to ourselves to defend the "self" or ego. We will lie also to others for the same reason. Various forms and types of deception become a way of life.

Although society allegedly frowns upon the act of lying, it accepts it in many of our interpersonal relationships such as in the areas of politics, advertising and social graces. Because of this, human beings become well conditioned to telling lies. They are told without any compunction. The ability to lie becomes a part of the total personality structure.

Too many investigators underestimate the capacity of human beings to lie. People who are guilty of a crime naturally do not tell the truth. They will attempt to defend themselves by lying until such time as the pain of their own conscience becomes unbearable or outside influences prompt them to reveal their guilt.

Confessions Induced

A completely voluntary confession is a myth. An individual confesses when he can no longer endure the pressure of his own conscience or what he construes to be a threat from an outside source. A guilty subject will continue to lie until such time as he believes that the benefits of telling the truth exceed those of lying.

The defense mechanisms that I discussed earlier are the personification of lying to oneself or to others. For your purposes, the human practice of telling a significant lie is important. By significant I mean a lie that is told in a controlled situation and where the subject is fearful of being found out. A controlled situation would be any place where if the subject were revealed as lying, he would suffer reprisals for his deception. Such places would be courtrooms, police stations, etc. It is the significant lie which reveals itself in behavioral signs.

We are all aware of the alleged behavioral symptoms of lying, such as various nervous mannerisms, a pulsation of the carotid artery, a dryness of the lips, etc. Without arguing the validity of these signs as indicating guilt, I can definitely state that they are based on the emotion of fear. It then becomes a question for the interrogator to differentiate those symptoms which arise out of fear as possessed by the guilty or the apprehensiveness of the innocent.

Lying Is "Hard Work"

Even more important than an understanding of these different behavioral signs is the knowledge that it requires greater mental energy to tell a lie than to tell the truth. To tell a significant lie in a controlled situation is work. It is the exertion of this additional mental energy and physical counterpart that best reveals the liar. The astute interrogator learns to recognize the struggling, halting, laborious efforts of the liar.

The truthful individual looks and sounds like he is telling the truth. The truthful individual exerts a certain degree of mental energy to recall events, but he is not burdened with the work of the liar who, being dependent upon imagination, must exert a great amount of mental energy.

Up to this point we have dealt with the study of behavioral signs which tend to indicate guilt. Determining the true guilty party is only half the job. It now becomes necessary to substantiate our opinion by eliciting a confession from the guilty party. When you consider that 75 percent of all convictions in criminal court proceedings are based upon confessions, you realize the importance of astute interrogation. That is why in my opinion interrogation is the most important aspect of criminal investigation. The truth of any given situation is contained in the minds of the people involved.

Guilty Best Informed

A valid confession brings us closer to the truth than any other means. All other investigation techniques allow us only to infer the truth. The guilty party is and always will be the best source of information. We must continue to study ways of eliciting the truth as it is contained in the minds of human beings.

Down through the years I have become aware that chances of obtaining confessions are based upon percentages. Less than one percent of confessions will be from people who do so without any prompting whatsoever. This is a rare occasion. I include this percentage only because it does happen once in a while.

Twenty percent of the guilty subjects you interrogate will confess because of the pain of their own conscience, despite the fact that you are unable to confront them with any evidence indicating their guilt. It is important to understand, however, that this 20 percent will not volunteer the truth until they are interrogated for a reasonable length of time.

You can increase your percentage of confessions from guilty parties if you are able to confront them with one or two good pieces of evidence. An exceptionally good interrogator utilizing the polygraph and all available evidence can obtain, as a rule, confessions from 75 percent of the guilty subjects he interrogates.

Some Never Confess

Twenty-five percent of your guilty subjects will not confess under any circumstances, regardless of the amount of evidence with which you confront them. These figures are based upon a statistical analysis of over 10,000 criminal interrogations conducted in the polygraph office of the Miami Police Department during an 8-year period. Don't let anyone kid you into thinking that, given sufficient evidence and unlimited time, you can obtain a confession from anyone. You can't do it. We have tried.

There are varied reasons why 25 percent of your guilty subjects will not confess under any circumstances. I have placed my personal label on seven different types of liars who make up this 25 percent category. I call them:

1. The Panic Liar
2. The Occupational Liar
3. The Tournament Liar
4. The Sadistic Liar
5. The Ethnological Liar
6. The Neurotic Liar
7. The Psychopathic Liar

The seven different types of liars represent those that I have most frequently encountered during my years of experience in interrogating thousands of individuals. Let us briefly examine each.

Fear of Confession

The Panic Liar lies because of an intense fear of the consequences of confessing. He cannot bear to face the shame of admitting his guilt. He finds his act so intolerable that he cannot accept guilt. He realizes the social consequences of his act. The thought of going to jail, the potential embarrassment he will face in front of friends and loved ones is too much for him to bear. Confessing would be too much of a blow to his ego. In essence the Panic Liar believes that by confessing he would only make a bad situation worse.

The Occupational Liar becomes proficient in the act of lying because of years of training and occupational necessity. It is not my intention to unjustly accuse certain occupations of practicing wholesale deception. The fact is, however, that certain members of various occupations who engage primarily in sales work become very proficient at deceiving their fellow man.

These individuals find the transition from lying to the general public to lying to those in a position of authority quite easy. A man who has made his living by lying for 20 or 30 years is a difficult subject to cope with during an interrogation. Through years of experience this subject has become a practiced liar and he is not about to change his ways just because he is talking to a person in a position of authority. Despite what you may be thinking, I have many other types of occupations in mind besides the stereotyped used car salesman.

Some Enjoy Lying

My third type, the Tournament Liar, is the one I most enjoy watching in operation. This is the person who loves to lie. To him it is a personal challenge and each person he lies to becomes a new conquest. He started out when he was first able to talk by deceiving his mother and father. He thrives on his ability to deceive people. To him it means power. But most of all he loves to lie under pressure. That is why I call him the Tournament Liar. Your interrogation of him is his biggest challenge. After all, he gets tired of lying to nobodies and you represent a new thrill.

Many of these individuals in a lax moment have related to me, "Mr. Holmes, I just don't get any kick out of telling the truth." To confess would be to admit defeat and this would be too much of a blow to his personal ego. Many mistakes have been made by investigators because they did not realize they were coping with this type of individual.

The Sadistic Liar lies because it is the only weapon he has left with which to fight. He realizes that there is sufficient evidence to convict him, but he is not going to give his investigators the satisfaction of hearing him confess. He is the martyr type. He is the one who goes to the electric chair still claiming that he is innocent. He feels sadistic delight in observing the controversy over his guilt or innocence. He even enjoys seeing his own family suffer by pretending that the police have incarcerated an innocent man. Denying his guilt is the only means he has for getting even with his so-called cruel world. Caryl Chessman was a prime example of this type of liar.

Taught By Parents

The next type is the Ethnological Liar. Certain subdivisions of mankind actually condone the parental teaching of children never to admit the truth to people in a position of authority. In other words, these parents teach their children that no one likes a "squealer."

This type of thinking probably had its inception back in the days of the feudal system in Europe. The vassals taught their children never to admit any wrongdoing to the lord of the land. They taught their children that if they ever were caught killing one of the lord's prized deer for food, not to admit their guilt regardless of the punishment inflicted upon them. The creed of the Mafia represents the personification of this type of thinking.

The Neurotic Liar exemplifies the basis of all neuroses in that the individual lies to himself. This individual cannot and will not accept guilt. Through the unconscious process of repression, the acceptance of guilt is blocked from the conscious mind. I have always stated, "Give me a subject who lies to me and I have a chance of breaking him, but not one who lies to himself." This subject will not accept the truth because it is too ego-shattering.

Ironically, this subject actually enjoys intensive interrogation in that it is viewed as a form of punishment and satisfies deep-rooted guilt feelings. On many occasions I have had this type of subject display general disappointment because the interrogation period had ended.

Psychopath the Toughest

The most difficult of all subjects is the Psychopathic Liar. The personality structure of the true psychopath is difficult to define.

Not all psychiatrists agree as to the underlying basis for this type of personality development. The degree of hereditary or environmental influence which has a bearing on this type of personality development is extremely difficult to establish.

For our purposes the most important aspect of their personality is the fact that they seem to be without conscience. They show no compunction for their acts of wrongdoing. In this respect they display no manifestations of guilt. This type of subject fools more investigators than any other type. They are persuasive talkers and ingratiating in nature. They will con you right out of your socks. Their basic personality make-up helps them to be effective liars. They have a complete disregard for the feelings of other human beings.

A sympathetic approach to this type of subject is useless. You can only hope that you have sufficient evidence to convict them without a confession. They are the greatest actors in the world, and even though you have overwhelming evidence indicating their guilt, their persuasiveness will make you doubt your own mind.

System Under Fire

There is a concerted effort in this country to eliminate the privilege of interrogation. The way things are going, eventually we will not be able to interrogate unless it is in the presence of the suspect's attorney. Recent court decisions placing more and more restrictions upon criminal interrogation are a dangerous trend.

Eliminating the opportunity to obtain confessions makes the crime problem almost unanswerable. We are not now winning the war against crime. We are only stemming the tide. Crime as a social problem is predicated upon human deception. We should have the right to question the nefarious mind that threatens its fellow man.

It is the job of government to insure human rights, but not to the point where it jeopardizes the general welfare. Ironically, those who are in favor of placing more and more restrictions upon criminal investigation and interrogation have created a crime problem so great that local law enforcement can no longer cope with it, and the thing they allegedly fear the most, a national police state, may come about to handle the problem. They are so naive concerning the social problem of crime that they do not realize this threat.

Warren D. Holmes

A nationally known polygraph examiner who has worked on major cases throughout the U.S., Mr. Holmes is president of Holmes Polygraph Service, Inc., Miami, Florida. A member of the Miami Police Department for 13 years and director of their polygraph bureau for nine years, Mr. Holmes has been an instructor in psychology and criminology at the Miami Police Academy, and in criminology at Miami's Dade County Junior College.

Mr. Holmes is a past president of the Academy of Scientific Interrogation (now the American Polygraph Association) and has written numerous articles on lie detection and interrogation. He has been a guest lecturer at many colleges on the art of interrogation.

Chapter 15

WHY PEOPLE CONFESS—
REFLECTIONS ON 1,000 INTERROGATIONS

By Roger K. Griffin

No one seems surprised when a confession is introduced if it is revealed that the suspect was caught in the act. The professional interrogator is often asked, however, to explain why a subject confesses when the evidence is circumstantial.

The question is asked with the implication that one would not confess to wrongdoing unless threatened with severe punishment or unless promised immunity or some other reward. The implication is just as often that the confession was obtained through the mistreatment of the subject, either psychological or physical.

I have recently reviewed 1,000 interrogations which I personally conducted over the past several years. These interrogations were the result of documented reports by shopping investigators under my direction that the subjects had failed to record sales on the cash register in the retail stores where they were employed.

In 75 percent of those cases, the subject admitted to the theft of unrecorded funds. Each confession included a written statement detailing the thefts in amounts up to $10,000. The extremely high percentage of confessions does raise a reasonable question of

©1970, 1975, Security World Publishing Co., Inc.

why those persons did admit theft.

I believe that the interrogator's success over a long period of time is directly proportional to how well he takes advantage of what he has available to him. I would like to examine some of those things, and try to relate them to the interrogator's success.

Human Nature

The things which the interrogator must rely upon can be separated into two different groups. The first group might be called the basic forces and impulses of human nature. When one asks the question, "Why does one confess?" one would as well ask, "What is the human being's basic need to confess?" The idea that such a need exists is not new. Confession is a sacrament of religion. Such a requirement could not be imposed upon the human spirit. The need had to exist first. "Confession is good for the soul" perhaps became a cliche because it is true.

No less an original thinker than Theodore Reik devoted a whole series of lectures to the subject. They are collected into a volume which bears the title *The Compulsion to Confess*. The difficulty with which secrets are kept demonstrates the need to tell what is within all of us.

I believe that every human being who does something wrong has a basic urge to tell someone about it. In some cases, the need would be that of the braggart to sustain his ego. In other cases, it would be the need for expiation. The latter, if true, is a basis for hope. It is easier to proceed if one believes that most people, most of the time, want to do what is right and are sorry for their wrongs.

These psychological forces are there for the interrogator to seek. They are the lock. The interrogator is the key. He cannot expect to become the master key which will fit every lock; but with application, experience, and understanding, he can increase his range.

The interrogator will not find these forces uniform in all of his subjects. He will be convinced that they are totally lacking in some. They are at best nebulous and, therefore, more a matter of feeling than fact. But now let us turn to the factual side of the interrogator's endeavor.

"Setting the Stage"

If the interrogator is unaware of the elements we have just

discussed, he can still be successful if he places proper emphasis on the details which he can control. We might call this aspect of the interrogator's job "setting the stage."

It is not possible to make an in-depth background investigation of the subject in the kind of cases we are discussing here. But in most cases, there is a wealth of information available about the subject if the interrogator takes the trouble to obtain it. The best source for this information is the subject's personnel file. Since you are working with officials of the subject's company, this file can be obtained with a minimum of effort. In a matter of moments you have a picture of the subject's previous and current work record. If the subject has been a disciplinary problem, or if he has received commendations, the file will reflect it, along with such pertinent facts as wage garnishments or judgments. A few moments' conversation with the subject's immediate superior will often provide information about personal habits, interests, and outside pursuits.

This kind of information provides a picture of the person the interrogator will deal with, and may determine the direction of the interrogator's approach. I have found that this information serves another, and perhaps more important, purpose. It enables the interrogator to identify with the subject as a person. It is simply more difficult to communicate with a total stranger than it is with someone you know something about.

Physical Setting

The physical setting for the interrogator and the subject is as important as any other aspect of the procedure. It is not possible to have a calm, businesslike conversation unless a private office or similar facility is made available. To communicate properly, the interrogator must be able to hold the subject's attention. Interruptions which divert the subject's attention and break the interrogator's line of thought can destroy all hope of establishing communication between the interrogator and the subject.

The interrogator's skill is based on his ability to recognize that certain aspects of human nature are working for him. His skill is further measured by how much importance he attaches to the details which surround the interrogation, and how successful he is in controlling those details. Proper evaluation of detail and proper attention to it will contribute much to the interrogator's success.

I believe that most interrogators will agree that some few subjects will confess to anyone who confronts them. This subject has a highly developed conscience or a very weak personality. I further believe, however, that most subjects confess because of the skill of the interrogator.

The use of skill does not suggest that the interrogator took unfair advantage of the subject. Neither does it suggest that devious methods were used to obtain the confession. In its purest form perhaps the interrogator's skill can be defined as his ability to talk with his subject. If the interrogator is self-conscious, embarrassed, or otherwise ill at ease when facing his subject, his uncertainty will be communicated to the subject, and his effectiveness will be lost.

The interrogator's professionalism is perhaps best measured by how he relates to his subject, how he views his role, and how well he knows himself. The most successful interrogator will have a feel for people. He will relate well to his subject and have compassion for him.

Chief Harold Cramer of the Los Angeles County Sheriff's Office has an outstanding reputation as an interrogator based on his results in difficult cases. He is also both articulate and generous in sharing his ideas with others in the field. I once heard him say that he cried honest tears when listening to a murderer relate the horrible events he had endured prior to the violence which led to his arrest. But compassion for the man and understanding why he reacted violently did not alter the fact that murder is against the law. During the same session, Inspector Cramer made a point I never shall forget: "Whether a person is successful and influential or the worst loser in San Quentin, what each one seeks is human understanding."

It is a mistake to feel righteous when confronting the subject of some wrongdoing. It is a mistake even to feel superior, because any man, regardless of the power of being right, must truly say, "There, but for the grace of God, go I."

Absence of Logic

To ask why a person confesses to theft is as academic as asking why a person steals. This idea interests me particularly because in the 1,000 cases I have referred to here, there is an absence of logic why the person stole in the first place. The facts in all cases were the same. The subject had failed to record on the cash register purchases made by shopping investigators. The failure to record has been observed and documented in affidavits on two or more different days, thereby establishing a pattern of behavior.

Out of these cases, only an insignificant few were what might be identified as criminal types. That is to say that, from what was known about them, they appeared to be people whose past pursuits were legitimate rather than criminal. The external reason they stole is obvious. The money was there. It was a simple matter not to record it on the cash register. The ease with which such a theft can be accomplished made the temptation too much to withstand. This explains the mechanics of the thefts, but not the character flaw which is the basis for such conduct.

In almost all of the confessions I have referred to, the person gave some reason for the theft. The reason was rarely volunteered. It came forth as a result of the subject being encouraged to explain, in human terms, why the thefts had occurred. The challenge to the interrogator is to communicate to the subject that he is truly interested in the subject's feelings.

There is a tendency to label the subject's explanation a rationalization; and, no doubt, it is purely that in some cases. The need to justify one's conduct or oneself is another constant force which can be relied upon.

Human Understanding

The consistency with which these explanations pour forth, and the eagerness with which the subject seizes the opportunity to express himself, reinforces Inspector Cramer's observation that we all seek human understanding. Sometimes when a subject believes that you want to listen, it becomes obvious that yours is the first sympathetic ear he has had in a long time. If you allow it, he will range far afield and tell you of troubles in no way connected with the theft.

It would be a mistake to leave the impression that all subjects can be neatly categorized or that one simple formula will enable the interrogator to reach each person he talks with. Each subject reacts and responds differently, and it is a mistake to read too much into the external facts one may know about a subject. The meekest looking subject may turn out to have a profanely colorful vocabulary, which he uses to tell you that he does not care to talk with you at all. But, even more often, the subject who has a reputation for being a troublemaker and a tough guy tells you with great feeling that he is relieved to be able to talk about his problems.

The interrogator must be prepared for the fact that some of his subjects will refuse to talk with him for reasons that are unknown. It may be a⁻ simple a matter as the interrogator's physical appearance or mannerism reminding the subject of ⁻omeone he dislikes or fears.

As in all human endeavor, the interrogator must be prepared for failure. Proper attention to detail and an understanding of human nature will, however, prepare the interrogator for a high degree of success.

The complete explanation of why a person confesses may never be made. A partial explanation appears, quite reasonably, to be that, when the interrogator creates the proper atmosphere and reaches his subject on the human level, a confession will be forthcoming.

Roger K. Griffin

Mr. Griffin is the General Manager of Commercial Service Systems, Inc., an investigative company which specializes in retail security systems for control of losses due to dishonest personnel, worthless checks and shoplifting. CSS is headquartered in Los Angeles and has divisional offices in Burlingame, California; Portland, Oregon; Seattle, Washington; Phoenix, Arizona; Dallas, Texas; and Houston, Texas.

Mr. Griffin is a veteran of World War II and the Korean War, and is a graduate of Westminster College, Fulton, Missouri, with a B.A. in political science. A past President of the Southern California Retail Special Agents Association, he is a member of the Southern California Check Investigators and the American Society for Industrial Security.

Chapter 16

CONFESSIONS AND SIGNED STATEMENTS

By Michael Invergo

Constitutional restrictions on the admissibility of confessions basically do not apply to private security personnel. However, I think security personnel should be familiar with the law, because there are times when they may take a statement or interrogate someone at the direction of a police officer. In this case, these constitutional restrictions will apply to the security officer. At other times a police officer may be present when the security officer questions someone, and by virtue of that officer's presence, the rules will apply.

Many police officers hold part-time jobs as store detectives and other security personnel. In this capacity, the rules set forth by the Supreme Court would apply; even though the officer would be questioning someone in his capacity as a private security officer, he is still a police officer. If another security officer is involved, then these rules will apply to him as well.

Thus there may be many instances in which these rules would apply to private security personnel. If security personnel are not

From a presentation given at the International Security Conference in Chicago, 1970 (revised 1975).

familiar with these rules, the statements they take will not be admissible in court.

Historical Court Decisions on Confessions

Historically, I would like to point out a few legal aspects of statements. The Supreme Court of the United States for many years never took cognizance of the fact that confessions were used in evidence against arrested persons. In 1936 *Brown vs. Mississippi* became the first major case in which the United States Supreme Court did recognize that confessions could be a problem in the law enforcement field.

In this case a Negro was arrested for the murder of a white man in Mississippi, and evidence at the trial indicated the officers had beaten and tarred and feathered him until he confessed. The confession was admitted in court as evidence against him. His attorney appealed all the way to the U.S. Supreme Court.

The first major rule to emerge from the Brown case was that in order for confessions to be admissible, they must be voluntary. Any confession which is obtained by physical duress or physical coercion would not be admissible in evidence, because it would not be voluntary. Because the court cannot rely on its trustworthiness, it should not be admissible against any person. The decision in the Brown case was reversed because of the physical abuse the defendant suffered in his interrogation by the police officers.

Later on, the court made additional rulings regarding voluntariness. Unnecessary delay between the time the suspect was arrested and the time he was taken before a judge or a magistrate was held to make a confession inadmissible. The first time the Supreme Court ever stated this rule was in 1943 in *McNabb vs. the United States.* The McNabb brothers were distillers of illegal alcohol, and federal agents had been after them for some time. They made a raid, and there was a shoot-out in which a federal officer was killed.

One of the McNabb brothers was arrested, and he was questioned for a long period of time, approximately three days. There was no evidence of physical abuse. There was no claim by the defendant of physical abuse; however, he was not taken before a judge for three days. He was questioned until finally he confessed, implicating his brothers and a few other people. Subsequently they were arrested, tried, and convicted at the trial level.

Their attorney appealed to the U.S. Supreme Court. The Court reversed the decision, setting forth the rule that an arrested person shall be taken before a judge or magistrate *without unnecessary delay*. The wording does not state a limit on the length of time an arrested person can be held for investigation. It merely says *without unnecessary delay*. If there is a *necessary* delay for purposes of investigation—line-ups, locating witnesses or whatever—this delay could justify a longer period of detention than would reasonably be necessary under normal circumstances.

What the Court said in this case was that any confession elicited from an arrested person during this illegal period of unnecessary detention will not be admissible. Any statement made after a long period of detention between the time of arrest and the time of going before a judge cannot be held as voluntary.

The McNabb case applied only to federal law enforcement officers for a number of years. However, the trend indicated that eventually the Court would impose the same rule on local police officers; thirteen years later, they did.

In 1957 the Mallory case was brought before the U.S. Supreme Court. The case involved a defendant accused of rape in Washington, D.C. Mr. Mallory was arrested and questioned for some seven hours before he was taken before a U.S. Commissioner. During this seven-hour period, he confessed.

Again, there was no claim or evidence of physical abuse, torture or beatings of any kind. It was simply a seven-hour delay between the time he was arrested and the time he was taken before a judge. At his trial he was convicted on the basis of his confession.

This case gave the Supreme Court an opportunity to impose the rule of unnecessary delay on local police. (A Washington, D.C. case is considered the same as a state case coming before the Court.) They reversed the Mallory decision and imposed the same rule on states as they had earlier in the McNabb case. Any arrested person must be taken before a judge without unnecessary delay. If a confession is obtained during an unnecessary delay, it will be inadmissible in court.

The Omnibus Crime Control and Safe Streets Act of 1968 amended the "unnecessary delay" rule. According to this law, unnecessary delay in bringing a suspect before a magistrate in and of itself does not render a confession inadmissible, but the delay is to be considered with all other surrounding facts and circumstances in determining voluntariness.

The Mallory rule was probably the most restrictive rule on police officers until the Miranda decision in 1966. It did not leave much time to hold an arrested person for investigation. He generally had to be booked and taken before a judge by the next court session. If a man was arrested at ten o'clock at night, he had to be in court for the most part by nine o'clock the next morning.

What the courts were really doing with the Brown, McNabb, and Mallory cases was warning police about abuses that were in violation of the Fifth Amendment. After all, that's what confessions are all about—the privilege against self-incrimination. The courts were saying over these years, "Officers, when you make an arrest, an arrested person has a right under the Fifth Amendment not to incriminate himself."

Certain abuses did exist in getting confessions. As in the Brown case, physical coercion sometimes took place. If confessions obtained following beatings were inadmissible, the motivation to beat suspects would be removed. Prior to the McNabb and Mallory rulings, it was not uncommon for an arrested person to be held as long as necessary to get a confession from him. Following the rulings, it was clear that if the confession would not be admissible in evidence under these conditions, there was little value in holding the suspect for a long period of time.

The effect of these decisions was to prevent certain abuses under the Constitution. Many practices were stopped. There had been a practice in many large cities of transporting a suspect in a murder, rape, burglary or robbery case from one station to another to prevent his family or lawyer from finding out where the prisoner was. This was done with interrogation in mind, consistently questioning the man in relays for as many as three, four, five days, until finally the man would break down and confess. This practice was eliminated on the federal level with the McNabb case and on the local level with the Mallory case.

Right to Presence of Counsel

In 1958, two murder cases in New York and California—the Cicinia and Crooker cases—both involved the same principle of law. In each case, the defendant surrendered to the police with his attorney. In each case the police, once having obtained custody of the defendant, refused to allow the attorney to be present at any interrogation. They refused to allow the attorneys to see their clients or give any advice. Confessions were obtained in both cases. Both Cicinia and Crooker were convicted, and both appealed at approximately the same time.

The lawyers' argument for the basis of appeal was that the defendants were denied their Constitutional right to assistance of counsel; that they had a right to see their lawyers and the police refused that right to them. The United States Supreme Court upheld the convictions, stating that the defendant's right to an attorney begins in the courtroom at the first court hearing, and not in the police station.

That was the law until 1964. In that year, Danny Escobedo was arrested in Chicago for murder. The police, following the rule of the Cicinia and Crooker cases, did not allow the defendant's lawyer to see his client. Police obtained a confession, although Escobedo refused to sign it. The confession was admitted in evidence against him at the trial, and he was convicted of murder.

He appealed to the Illinois Supreme Court, which upheld the decision, stating the police did not violate any Constitutional rights of the defendant. Escobedo's lawyer took the case to the U.S. Supreme Court. In 1958 the Court had said that a defendant did not have a right to see his lawyer in a police station; but in 1964 they reversed themselves and said that Escobedo's rights had been violated; the police should have allowed the attorney to be present during the interrogation.

In the Escobedo decision, the Court also stated that the defendant's right to an attorney becomes effective when an investigation proceeds from the "investigatory stage to the accusatory stage." In other words, when the police are making an investigation and do not yet have any suspect in mind, then they don't have to allow any of the people under investigation the right to see a lawyer. But once the investigation turns to an accusatory stage, where the police are now focusing on investigation of one particular individual, then the right to an attorney applies.

The Miranda Decision

Although the Escobedo case also mentioned the suspect's right to remain silent and his right to know that anything he says may be used against him, the decision was vague in these areas. Two years later, in 1966, the vagueness was clarified when the Supreme Court decided the Miranda case. *Miranda* is probably the most famous confession case of all time, because it is the most restrictive since the Supreme Court started deciding cases dealing with confessions. In the Miranda case, the court made a lot of statements and gave a lot of rules to follow.

The court said that when a person was arrested, no one was protecting the Fifth Amendment rights of the arrested person. Certainly the police were not protecting them—the police were interested in gathering evidence necessary for conviction. Since no one was looking after this person's rights, the court imposed upon the police the obligation to protect these rights. The Court stated that any person arrested or otherwise deprived of his freedom of movement[5] shall not be questioned or interrogated unless he has been fully advised of his rights and unless he makes a knowing, intelligent, voluntary waiver of those rights. Then and only then can he be questioned; then and only then will anything he says be admissible as evidence against him in court.

The Miranda decision outlined four things that the defendant must be informed of:

1.   He must be told he has a right to remain silent. That right is absolute. He doesn't have to say anything, not even his name.

2.   He must be told that anything he does say can and *will* be used as evidence against him in a court of law. If he is not told this, his statement will be rendered involuntary.

3.   He must be advised that he has a right to have his lawyer present during any questioning. If he has a lawyer, he must be allowed to call the lawyer, who must be given a reasonable amount of time to arrive at the station. This right necessarily implies the Sixth Amendment right to assistance of counsel, which means that the lawyer must be allowed to talk to the defendant for a little while before he is questioned. (Naturally, any good lawyer will tell him to give his name and address only and answer no questions.)

4.   He must be told that if he cannot afford a lawyer, one will

---

[5] According to the Court, a person is deprived of his freedom of movement when he becomes a suspect in a case, whether or not he is arrested.

be appointed for him if he so desires. If he replies that he does want a lawyer, no interrogation can take place until one arrives.

These four things must be made known to him, and in such a manner that he understands them. It is not sufficient merely to tell him these things or read them from a card, as many policemen and federal agents do. He must understand them.

For example, if a motion to suppress confession is made in court, the attorney will ask the arresting officer what he advised the defendant and whether the defendant understood. Factors such as the defendant's educational background will come into play, as well as his sobriety and mental condition. If a man was drunk or has very little education, the court might feel he did not really understand what he was told.

Once the suspect understands these rights, he may waive them voluntarily, if he does so *knowingly* and *intelligently*. Again, the decision on whether the waiver was made voluntarily and intelligently will depend upon his educational background, his sobriety, mental condition, and so forth.

Chief Justice Earl Warren, who wrote the decision in the Miranda case, stated that the prosecution has a heavy burden of proof regarding a voluntary waiver. A defense attorney may argue that a waiver was not voluntary by establishing the fact that a number of armed police officers were present at the time, thus creating a "psychological coercion." Many courts, in fact, have found that no waiver can be truly voluntary if it is made while the individual is in police custody.

In short, in order for a confession to be admissible in court, the defendant must have received and understood the four warnings, and voluntarily and intelligently waived his rights.

Miranda Modifications

There have been several U.S. Supreme Court decisions since the Miranda case that should be considered here.

In *Orozco vs. Texas* (1968), a murder suspect was questioned by the police at his home in the early morning hours. No Miranda warnings were given. The Texas Supreme Court affirmed the conviction, holding that the confession was admissible since it was obtained in a "non-custodial setting."

The U.S. Supreme Court reversed the conviction. Since the investigation focused on Orozco, the court held, the confession was obtained in a "custodial setting" and was therefore inadmissible because the Miranda rules were not followed.

The restrictiveness of the Miranda rules was modified somewhat by *Harris vs. New York* (1971). Arrested for a narcotics violation, Harris confessed while in custody. He had not been informed of his Miranda rights. Thus, the confession could not be used in evidence at the trial. Harris testified in his own behalf, denying the charges. For the purpose of impeaching the defendant, the arresting officer testified as to the confession Harris had made.

The U.S. Supreme Court affirmed the conviction, holding that a statement which is inadmissible because of failure to give the Miranda warnings, but which is in all other respects voluntary, can be used to impeach the testimony of the person making the statement.

The Harris decision was reinforced by the U.S. Supreme Court in *Hass vs. Oregon* (1975). Charged with theft, Hass was given the Miranda warnings. Although he asked for a lawyer, the police continued to question him without obtaining an attorney. Hass made some incriminating statements, which could not be used at the trial. However, a police officer testified to these incriminating statements for the purpose of impeaching Hass's testimony during the trial. The U.S. Supreme Court affirmed the conviction, citing *Harris.*

Rules of Evidence

A basic understanding of some of the rules of evidence is necessary in discussing confessions and statements.

Confessions fall into the category of hearsay in the rules of evidence. Hearsay is any testimony by a witness as to what someone else told him. A confession or admission is hearsay because the officer who took the confession would be testifying in court to what somebody else (the defendant) told him. Generally, hearsay is inadmissible in court because it tends to be untrustworthy and unreliable, but there are certain types of hearsay which are admissible.

Confessions and admissions are exceptions to the hearsay rule. Because the courts have found that confessions and admissions are reliable, they are admissible as evidence. A person will not generally make a statement against his own self-interest unless it is true. There are exceptions, of course, and the courts realize this. But under this theory, a confession or admission made against a person's own self-interest would be considered trustworthy and reliable, even though it is hearsay.

Terms Defined

A *confession* is defined as a complete acknowledgement of guilt or participation in a criminal offense. Confessions fall into two categories: judicial and extra-judicial. A judicial confession is a plea of guilty in open court. The extra-judicial confession, the one that most concerns us here, is one made outside of court. This is the confession made to a police officer, security officer, priest, wife, brother, friend. Any confession made to any of these people is considered an extra-judicial confession. If it is made to other than a police officer, then the rules we've been talking about do not apply. If the confession is made to a police officer, or *at the direction of a police officer*, then the rules do apply.

An *admission* is a declaration against self-interest; however, it is merely any incriminating statement. A person may deny guilt yet make some sort of an admission; he may state, "I did not commit the murder, but the gun lying beside the body belongs to me." That's an admission. Although denying the murder, he is making an admission, even though the statement may deny actual participation in the crime. The rules apply to admissions as they do to confessions.

An *exculpatory statement* is one in which a person admits he did what he is charged with, but gives a legal excuse for doing it. For example, "I killed John Doe, but I killed him in self-defense," would be an exculpatory statement. The Miranda rules apply to exculpatory statements. An exculpatory statement cannot be used in court unless the prosecution can show that the defendant was advised of his rights, understood his rights, and waived them.

In other words, any statement of any kind whatsoever from an arrested person will not be admissible against him unless the rules of the Miranda case are followed, and proven in court prior to the introduction of the confession into evidence.

Volunteered Statements

Up to this point we have covered only the legal requirements for voluntary statements obtained through interrogation. Let us turn now to *volunteered statements*, where these rules do not apply.

For example, a man may walk into a police station and say to the desk sergeant, "Three weeks ago I murdered my wife and buried her in the backyard. It's been bothering my conscience ever since; I think I should be punished for it." Must the desk sergeant stop this man and say, "Wait, I have to advise you of your rights, I can't listen to what you're saying"? The answer is, of course not. The man is volunteering this information. He is not under arrest or custody, or even a suspect. He has volunteered this statement, and the police can let him continue until he is through talking. At this point they would place him under arrest. In any further questioning of this man, the Miranda rules would have to be followed.

The same thing could happen when a police officer answers a call concerning a family disturbance. He walks into the apartment and finds a woman lying on the floor dead and a man standing there with a gun in his hand. The policeman asks, "What happened?" The man says, "I killed her, and I'm glad I did." This would be a good confession. It has been volunteered. Any admission, confession or incriminating statement given to a policeman making a general on-the-scene investigation of any incident is a good statement.

Structure of the Written Statement

There are a number of reasons why statements—not only of suspects or arrestees, but even of witnesses—should be put into writing in formal statements.

1.   A statement may clear up some other crime or provide additional information. Oral statements are as admissible in court as written statements, if their voluntariness can be demonstrated, but a written statement ties the knot a little more neatly.

2.   Another good reason for taking a statement, even from witnesses, is for impeachment purposes. To impeach means to discredit a witness. An individual may make a statement and, several months later, when it comes time for court, he changes his story complete-

ly. If a written, signed statement was made, his testimony can be impeached.

3.   Another reason for taking a written statement is that it discourages people from changing their stories. A person who has given a written statement, read and signed it, will hesitate to change his testimony later in court. He will be afraid of perjury charges or embarrassment.

Background Knowledge Needed

Before an officer takes a statement, he should have a good background knowledge of the case. He should know all the facts of the case, the little ones as well as the big ones. He should review all prior reports on the case. This makes it more difficult for the person giving the statement to deceive the officer taking the statement.

The officer should know as much as possible about the person he is taking the statement from. If he is an employee of the company the officer works for and is either a witness or a suspect in some theft or embezzlement, his personnel file will give good background on him. The officer should know his educational background, where he lives, his marital status, whether he served in the armed forces, what his prior job experience has been. A check should be made with the local police department for a criminal record.

A very basic rule in taking a statement is that it should be done in private. One or two disinterested witnesses should be present when the statement is taken, but no others. Statements should not be taken in places where there are many interruptions, where the phone is ringing, where people are walking in and out. These interruptions are very distracting and will interfere with the taking of the statement. The subject will offer less cooperation and give poor answers.

If the subject is a female, of course, a female should be present when the statement is taken.

Form of Statements

There are several forms of statements that may be used. The statement can be made as narrative by the person in his own writing, or dictated to the officer. It can be made in question-and-answer form, where the officer asks a question and the subject answers. I prefer a combination of the question-and-answer and narrative forms. Whatever form is used, the statement should be typed by the officer or his stenographer.

It is important to include in a written statement all elements of the offense in the defendant's own words.

For example, in a case of employee theft, the statement should not stop with the statement, "Yes, I took the television sets from the warehouse on such and such a date." When the subject is finished with his narrative portion of the statement, the officer should ask what he was going to do with those television sets. His answer will establish the intent element necessary in a theft or larceny case. Through his questions, the officer should be sure to include all elements of the crime in the statement.

The statement should begin with a general heading. "Statement being taken at such and such an address, in such and such a room, on such a date and at such a time." Those present should be listed. "This is the statement of John Smith, in relation to: theft," etc. The first question should be: "What is your name?" "What is your address?" "Whom do you live with?" "Are you married?" "What is your education?" The next question after these preliminary ones should be, "Do you know why you're here making a statement?" The answer will probably be, "Yes, I was involved in stealing some stuff from the warehouse," or something to that effect.

The officer should then initiate the narrative portion of the statement. . . "Tell me in your own words what happened." The suspect then relates, without interruption, exactly what he wants to say. When he is through, the officer must clarify anything that is ambiguous or vague.

A few intentional errors should be included in the statement. If the subject said he has three children, for example, the number might be changed to four in the statement. When the statement is finished, the subject must read it before he signs it. (The closing statements will include that he has read the document, consisting of so many pages, and he finds it to be true and correct, and therefore signs it.) When he notices the intentional errors, he will cross them out and insert the correct information. If at least one error is made on each page, it will help in court to show that he did in fact read the statement, that he made those corrections and no other corrections. This also helps to show voluntariness of the statement.

The suspect should not be asked in the statement whether he has previously been arrested for this offense. There is a well-grounded rule of evidence that no prior arrests or convictions are admissible against any defendant, because they tend to be pre-judicial.

If the individual is suspected of a number of offenses, separate statements should be taken for each offense, unless it can be established definitely that the several offenses were the result of one continuing act—what is called the "same conduct" in law. For example, a man breaks into a house to commit a theft. While in the house, he rapes and murders a woman. While leaving the house, the burglar sees the woman's husband coming home and kills him also. He has committed a burglary, a theft, a rape, and two murders, all from the result of the same conduct. One statement could include all those offenses.

If, however, there are several different acts of theft, or several different offenses, a separate statement must be obtained for each one. For example, if an employee in a department store says that on Monday he took a wrist watch, on Tuesday he took a diamond ring, and on Wednesday he took a portable radio, these are three separate crimes. If they are all put into one statement, its admissibility will be destroyed.

The foregoing is only a brief review of the constitutional restrictions affecting confessions and signed statements, and accepted practices in taking such statements. A thorough knowledge and understanding of them is essential for any security officer who might be involved in investigations and interrogations; only then can he be certain that the evolving body of law governing confessions and statements can work for him, not against him.

Michael Invergo

Sgt. Invergo joined the Chicago Park District Police in 1957, after having served as Chief Investigator for the Public Defender of Cook County for four years. When the Park Police merged with the Chicago Police Department, he was assigned to patrol duty. In 1961 he was promoted to detective and assigned to the Robbery

Section, where he remained until his promotion to sergeant in 1966. He has been an instructor in criminal law since 1966.

He served in the U.S. Army from 1953 to 1955, and was assigned to the Military Police. He received his Ph.B. from DePaul University in 1961, and attended DePaul University College of Law from 1961 to 1963.

VI.
THE
POLYGRAPH
AND
ITS USE

Chapter 17

THE USE OF THE POLYGRAPH
IN PRIVATE BUSINESS

By Lee Chandler

During the past few years, a great deal of discussion has taken place about the polygraph. Because it has come into such wide use in private business, the polygraph is of interest to almost everyone. It is possible that anyone, no matter his occupation or station in life, may at some time find it desirable to seek the services of a polygraph examiner. And it is especially essential that the security officer be thoroughly acquainted with the device.

Unfortunately, wide discussion of the polygraph has gotten far ahead of good sources of information. It is most common for people discussing the subject to state opinions without any working knowledge of either the instrument or the technique. The polygraph is a scientific instrument; using it is a specialized field that must be studied at length to fully comprehend its advantages and limitations. Still, many laymen form their opinions about it from listening to other laymen. The well-informed, security-oriented individual can be of tremendous help in this area.

It is unfortunate that during the early development of the polygraph, the term "lie detector" came into use. Not only is the term

© 1964, 1975, Security World Publishing Co., Inc.

inaccurate, but it is bad psychologically. The word "polygraph" is taken from the Greek, and means "many pictures"; that is, two or more recordings of various measurements. However, the most commonly used instruments measure and record three or more physiological responses.

A "lie detector," on the other hand, may be anything from a suspicious wife who questions her husband's alibis, to a simple electronic gadget that measures changes in the skin conductivity at the moment of some outside stimulus. *Neither* of the above "lie detectors" should be depended upon for accurate judgment *at all times.*

Training Important

The accuracy of any decision made from the polygraph examination depends 100% upon the qualifications, training and experience of the examiner. The instrument itself is not capable of being inaccurate. It is either working properly or is not working at all. There are a number of accredited schools for training polygraph examiners. These schools normally require some background in human relations, psychology, physiology, interviewing, investigation, legal aspects, mechanics of the instrument and many other phases of training necessary to acquire competency in polygraphy. Each of these schools issues a certificate of completion to those students who successfully accomplish the required achievements in their studies. In addition, most of these schools require a minimum of 150 supervised examinations after completion of the course, to be performed to the satisfaction of an already qualified expert, before issuing a final certificate.

There has been a considerable amount of confusion about the polygraph profession due to mistakes made by untrained persons using other than polygraph instruments, to form an opinion of whether a statement made by a person was truthful or not. The only opinions that should be considered as examples of the accuracy of any given polygraph evaluation should be those conducted by a qualified examiner utilizing standard polygraph equipment.

Much of the misinformation that has reached the public about the polygraph profession has been based on a lack of knowledge on the subject. Among these have been the various normal applications of the polygraph in private industry and business. Such things as background checking of job applicants utilizing the polygraph, setting up periodic testing of persons working in highly sensitive positions to prevent problems from occurring, and investigation of specific losses within a company structure to establish responsibility for an act against the company and fellow employees, are the normal application of the technique in private business. When properly introduced into any business, utilizing the services of qualified polygraph examiners, each of these applications serves a unique and desirable purpose. Only misconceptions of these applications offer resistance to such utilization.

The primary purpose of the polygraph in private business is to provide the subject of the test an objective and accurate means of verifying truthful statements about his actions or background. The polygraph becomes a lie detector only when the person taking the examination causes it to. In order to clarify some of the misconceptions about such utilization, look at some actual case histories where the polygraph has served a positive purpose:

As all polygraph evaluations in private situations are confidential, no names, locations, dates, or occupations will be included in these case histories.

Case # 1: Pre-Screening of Job Applicants

The owner of a business that, by its nature, caters to children had received a prescription from his doctor for some narcotic pills to ease the pain of a peptic ulcer. The man felt that the number of pills prescribed was insufficient to last until another prescription could be drawn from the doctor. Due to the intensity of the pain, the patient, although wrong in doing so, increased the number of pills designated on the prescription blank. He was subsequently arrested for forgery of a narcotics prescription.

The courts, hearing the story, put him on six months' probation, but local public sentiment sentenced the man to loss of his business, reputation and home. It was taken for granted by the public that the man had no doubt been selling narcotic pills to children. He was forced to leave the area of the country where he had lived and worked all his life, to seek a new life elsewhere. In applying for the better jobs in his new location, he again ran into subjective opinion. In the first three places of application he was hired for a short time, only to be "laid off" when his arrest record was learned. Now the employers were taking it for granted that he was an addict.

In one last attempt to get a job for which he was qualified, the man applied by making written application, excluding the arrest from the application form. To his dismay, the company asked him to verify his application in a polygraph evaluation. The man went to the examiner, fearful that the prior arrest would be detected and his last chance would be lost. Sure enough, the examination indicated deception regarding answers about prior arrests and narcotics use.

The man broke down and told the full story to the examiner, thinking all the time that there was no chance he would get the position he was seeking. The examiner asked the man if he would agree to answer questions regarding present use of narcotics and if he had ever sold any narcotic to any other person. The man agreed and was cleared of both situations. The ulcer had since been cured and no further use even of prescribed narcotics was necessary. The man did get the job because of the polygraph. He was turned down by the companies that did not use it.

Unlike the general belief that the polygraph evaluation of job applicants prevents people from getting good positions, past mistakes do not preclude the applicant from getting the position. The polygraph is merely used to establish that the person has learned by his past mistakes and is no longer making the same mistakes again and again. It verifies the qualifications that the good applicant is anxious to establish and prevents a less qualified applicant from taking the position only because he did a better job of covering up the derogatory part of his background by grossly falsifying the application and listing only references that he knows will paint a good picture of him.

Case # 2: Testing in Specific Loss Situations

A substantial amount of money mysteriously disappeared from the safe of a company. Five employees had an opportunity, through their normal handling of company funds, to take the money. All five denied any knowledge of the theft. Investigation proved only that no outside person could have caused the disappearance of the funds. Each of the five persons had need for money. No one person stood out as an obvious suspect.

Morale among the employees dropped to a seriously low level. The employees who were not involved were at a loss to know how to prove their innocence, although no one had been pointed out for individual suspicion. The insurance company suggested polygraph testing. Four of the employees agreed and were cleared of any suspicion in the matter. The fifth came under further investigation by the insurance investigators and sufficient evidence was gathered to indicate that he was the person who took the money. He subsequently admitted the theft.

The four persons who had lived under this veil of suspicion for several weeks knew nothing about the polygraph until that time. They were nervous about taking the test at first, not knowing what it was all about, but they thank the polygraph profession now for providing this much needed scientific means of clearing the innocent.

Case # 3: Testing to Prevent Problems

A small business was about to go broke and close because of a lack of profit. The location was good and should have attracted a fair trade. There was one owner and three employees. As a last resort, the owner turned to a polygraph program on a periodic testing basis. Each employee was offered complete immunity from any punishment for past misdeeds on the job if he would be loyal enough to come in and admit his past mistakes and have them verified as no more serious than he had stated. Each employee was instructed that the tests were completely voluntary and that they would only be expected to stop any theft activity from that time on.

During the testing procedures, each man admitted thefts in varying degrees, each thinking that he was the only one doing it, so therefore it would not be hurting the company. None of them realized that, collectively, they were running the company into bankruptcy. The company has since shown a good profit, resulting in higher wages and other benefits for the same employees.

Strangely enough, the owner was amazed at the increase in morale after the program went into effect. Members of the polygraph profession regularly see this improvement in morale when the company sets up sufficient controls to prevent such problems and all past problems are laid out to be recognized and corrected.

The average employee does not want to steal and resents his boss for allowing it. They welcome an adequate reason to have to stop.

The three cases listed are examples of situations that are seen every day in the polygraph profession. The qualified experts in the field know what a properly presented program can do for any business.

There are many good applications of the polygraph readily available to private business and private persons. Qualifications of the examiner and type of instruments used are paramount in getting good results. If you have questions about the polygraph, seek the advice of an expert in the field. There is no logic in obtaining information from other sources which may have only unknowledgeable opinions to offer. Know what the polygraph is before you discard a service that may be of value to you, as a security officer, and to your employer.

Lee Chandler

At the time this article was written, Mr. Chandler was general manager of Personnel Research and Development, Long Beach, Calif. He was secretary of the International Association of Polygraph Examiners (forerunner of the American Polygraph Association).

Chapter 18

THE POLYGRAPHIST AND HIS TEST

Edited by J. Kirk Barefoot

The polygraph technique had its beginnings in law enforcement in the Berkeley Police Department back in 1921. Since then, its use as an aid in official investigations has spread throughout the country, not only to large police departments but to medium-sized and small ones as well. Police officials agree that tremendous savings in manpower and money have resulted from the use of the polygraph technique to pinpoint criminal suspects and to clear innocent persons.

The biggest beneficiary of the polygraph has probably been the average citizen. Most police departments, placing great faith in the technique, will not press forward with the prosecution of a suspect

From "The Polygraph Story," edited by J. Kirk Barefoot; Authors: Stanley Abrams, J. Kirk Barefoot, Lynn P. Marcy, Raymond J. Weir, Charles H. Zimmerman, Lincoln M. Zonn; Contributors: Richard O. Arther, C. B. Hanscom, Leonard H. Harrelson, Carl S. Klump, Charles F. Marino, Richard D. Paterson, John E. Reid, W.A. Van de Werken. Copyright 1974, American Polygraph Association. Revised Third Printing October, 1974. Reprinted with permission of the American Polygraph Association. Copies of "The Polygraph Story" can be obtained from: American Polygraph Association, c/o J. Kirk Barefoot, 510 Fifth Ave., New York, N.Y. 10036.

who, though a prime candidate because of circumstantial evidence, has been cleared by the polygraph. It cannot be emphasized too strongly that thousands and thousands of Americans have been released from police custody and spared public prosecution because their innocence has been verified by the polygraph. Morever, not a single case has been found in which an innocent person was convicted because of polygraph error.

The Federal Government entered the polygraph field in the early 1940s when Frank A. Seckler, a Secret Service agent, was dispatched to Chicago to learn the technique from Leonarde Keeler. Seckler was the forerunner of more than a thousand federal employees who were to follow.

Initially the training of government polygraphists consisted of two or three months' instruction under the personal direction of Keeler himself. Later the training was formalized when Keeler established what is still known as the Keeler Polygraph Institute in Chicago. In the 1950s a military polygraph school was set up at Fort Gordon; today it trains the vast majority of military and government examiners, and is rated one of the top polygraph institutions in the country by the American Polygraph Association.

Private and Corporate Testing

The area of greatest growth in the polygraph profession during the 1960s was in the field of private and corporate testing. Most polygraphists in this category are employed either in one-man laboratories or in larger firms that may employ upwards of 35 staff examiners. A few large corporations have found it economical to employ their own in-house polygraph staffs, but such company examiners probably total no more than a hundred.

Some three thousand persons have been trained as polygraphists over the years; it is believed that there are about 1,500 in active practice today. Approximately one thousand are members of the American Polygraph Association. The majority of the rest belong to state associations, some of which are affiliated with the APA. The Association estimated that these 1,500 polygraphists will administer between 250,000 and 350,000 tests during 1975 (these figures include tests of all kinds, including those by law enforcement agencies). Better than 60 percent of the persons tested will be found truthful and cleared of false accusations or unjust suspicions. This means that annually more than 150,000 men and women have a very personal stake in preserving the polygraph technique, so that their reputations, jobs and the public safety and welfare can be protected.

Industries served by polygraphists are for the most part in the distribution, retailing and service categories. Among them are armored car services, airlines, retail and wholesale drug companies and drug manufacturers, department and other retail stores, the trucking industry, private guard services, restaurant chains, hotels, banks and brokerage houses, automobile rental firms, wholesale and retail liquor dealers, vending machine companies and finance companies—all businesses where large amounts of cash or valuable merchandise may present irresistible temptations.

The majority of such companies would use pre-employment polygraph screening; some would use the polygraph technique only in investigating specific instances of theft; a few would use it in periodic screening of currently employed persons. Some firms use two of the above approaches; some use all three.

The Test

In private testing for commercial firms, examinations are given either "on location" or in the polygraphist's own private polygraph suite. On-site examinations are almost always administered in a private office or conference room. The setting should be private and generally free from all distracting influences. The normal background noises to which the employee may be accustomed, however, are not considered an unfavorable influence on the test.

When the examinations are administered at the polygraphist's own laboratory, however, extra measures are taken to insure that no distractions are present, because here the examinee is in an unfamiliar environment and can be distracted more easily than on his home ground. Therefore, the person to be examined will usually encounter a scene something like this:

The polygraphist's waiting room is usually similar to the waiting room of any professional person such as a doctor, dentist, psychologist, etc. The decor of the waiting room is pleasant in nature and may or may not include some plant life, an aquarium, some background music, and reading material. The reading material in some cases may be a mixture of current periodicals along with some reading pieces on the polygraph test itself.

Normally, the person will be greeted by a receptionist upon

entering the suite of offices. This receptionist may or may not be in the immediate presence of the waiting room, depending upon the physical layout of the suite of offices. Contrary to charges made by polygraph antagonists, the duties of the secretary or receptionist do not include compiling data on the examinees who are waiting for the test. The end result of the examination procedure will be based on the results of the tests alone and the dialogue between the examiner and the examinee, not upon any impressions of a nonprofessional receptionist.

Physical Surroundings

The examination room itself is more austere in nature than the waiting room. It is almost always devoid of pictures, paintings or undraped windows. It is usually sound-proof in nature and with adequate carpeting on the floor. Normally, the furniture in such a room consists of the examination desk in which the polygraph instrument is recessed, the polygraphist's chair, and the examination chair, which may be of special design. The examination chair may range from an upright chair with what appear to be oversized arm rests, to a modified reclining chair, depending upon the individual preference of the polygraphist. Occasionally, the examination room may also contain a schoolroom type chair with writing arm which is used by the polygraphist in conducting his face-to-face pre-test interview.

In some cases, the examination room will also contain a one-way mirror opening onto an adjoining observation room together with a sound system connected to the observation room. The purpose of the mirror and the sound is for the training of polygraph interns and is no different in purpose from similar setups found in psychological testing laboratories and medical schools. Where such an arrangement is present, the examinee is so advised in the written release which he is requested to sign. In the event that the examinee should find the mirror and the sound objectionable, the polygraphist can render them inoperative.

Attachments

Upon entering the examination room, the examinee is usually introduced to and greeted by the polygraphist. Normally, he will be asked to sit in the examination chair and, depending upon the preference of the examiner, the examinee may be at that time immediately connected to the attachments of the instrument. These attachments, if connected immediately, are not activated during the pre-test interview. Other polygraphists prefer to conduct the pre-test interview prior to placing the attachments on the subject.

The first attachment that the examinee should expect to encounter is the blood pressure cuff, which is identical to that used by the physician, and which is attached to either the upper arm, the forearm, or in some cases the wrist. During the actual examination, this cuff is inflated to a medium pressure between the subject's systolic and diastolic blood pressure levels. Some persons report a mild amount of discomfort during the period of inflation, none of which is actually painful.

The second attachment consists of one or two rubber tubes which are placed around the trunk of the body. If only one tube is used, it is placed over the area of greatest movement during the respiration cycle. In some cases, two rubber tubes are used simultaneously to cover the upper and lower chest areas. The tubing is not uncomfortable in any way and simply measures and records, through the instrument, the rate and pattern of respiration.

The third attachment is usually placed on either one or two fingers, or through a dual connection with the palm of the hand. This attachment measures the changes in electrical resistance of the skin. There is absolutely no feeling of discomfort with this attachment.

Types of Techniques

It is not the purpose of this manuscript to serve as a definitive technical paper on the various types of tests used by polygraphists. It should be sufficient to enumerate the different types of tests the average layman is apt to encounter. For a technical review, the reader is referred to the literature of the field and to brochures published by the various polygraph training schools.

Major types of techniques are:

1. The Reid Control-Question Technique
2. The Backster/Zone of Comparison Technique
3. The Arther Technique

4. The Keeler Technique
5. The Integrated Control-Question Technique
6. The Hanscom Technique

The above techniques are generally used in what is known as specific tests—that is, where a loss has occurred or a crime has been committed. They differ in relatively minor procedural areas but are basically alike in attention to the psycho-physiological essentials. It is important for the reader to realize that most of the above techniques contain built-in safeguards for the person taking the test. One example of such a safeguard would be the use of a "guilt complex" question which is designed to identify the very rare person who will respond as if guilty to any type of pertinent question.

The most important safeguard, however, and one common to most polygraph techniques, is the use of one or more control questions throughout the test. A control question is one designed to create the probability that the subject will lie, or at least be unsure of complete truthfulness of his answer. It should be a question which is of no great significance and not particularly germane to the issue at hand. The examiner can utilize the response to a control question for comparison purposes to responses or lack of responses to relevant questions on the test. It is in this way that deception is detected. Even more important, truthfulness to relevant questions can be verified. Obviously, the use of such a question precludes an individual who is physiologically or psychologically incapable of responding from successfully passing the test procedure. In a case of this type, the verdict of the polygraphist would be "inconclusive." Such a result simply means that it is the same as if no test had been administered.

One of the oldest type of tests, but still probably the most reliable when administered under proper circumstances, is the so-called Peak of Tension test (P.O.T.). This is more commonly found in police testing and is used in conjunction with and as a follow-up to the earlier mentioned specific types of testing. The most commonly used P.O.T. test is based on a knowledge of the crime which can only be known by the perpetrator. As long as there is no widespread publicity about a crime, where intimate details as to the method of commission are known, it will be possible to devise a valid P.O.T. test.

An example of the P.O.T. test would be where the questions dealt with the caliber of the gun that was used in the commission of a homicide. Supposedly, the caliber of the gun would be known only to the perpetrator, and therefore suitable questions could be framed using various gun calibers. The P.O.T. test is infrequently used in private testing as the types of situations handled by the private polygraphist, as a rule, do not lend themselves to this type of test.

The Control Test

In order to aid in getting the examinee accustomed to the instrument, and also to develop some insight as to the reaction pattern of the person being tested, many polygraphists administer a control test prior to a specific examination or even prior to a pre-employment test.

The most typical control test likely to be encountered is the situation where the examinee has been requested to select a playing card or possibly a flinch card from five or seven presented to him. Normally, the cards are placed face down and only the subject knows which card was selected. The subject is then requested to answer "no" to all questions and an examination is then started. The examiner will run through each of the cards, asking the subject, "Did you choose card number _____?" Obviously, if all of the answers are "no," one answer is a lie.

Each subject has his own way of responding to deception while attached to the polygraph instrument, and in this way the polygraphist can get some idea beforehand in what manner the subject may respond if he resorts to deception. The control test itself is never compared to a subsequent examination for the purpose of diagnosing deception. This can only be done when the questions from the control test are later utilized and interspersed with other relevant questions.

The bulk of the work of the private polygraphist is divided between the periodic test and the most widely used, the pre-employment test. In the periodic test, normally administered to employees, questions are limited to a narrow range of issues pertaining to the handling of merchandise or money of the employer and all questions are usually prefaced with, "Since your last polygraph test, have you _____?" These tests are usually very narrow in scope, as there is no need to verify broader areas already covered by the pre-employment test.

The Pre-Employment Test

The pre-employment test accounts for the vast majority of all tests administered in the country today. As such, it has probably become the most controversial of all the tests given, and is probably the chief target of organized labor's thrust against the polygraph profession.

Many people fail to realize that a valid polygraph examination cannot be administered without prior discussion between the examiner and the examinee of the issues to be covered. Of the typical hour-long pre-employment test, 40 to 45 minutes is spent in what is called the pre-test interview. It is during this interview that the examinee's background, medical history and present physical condition are reviewed, in relation to the questions to be asked. The examinee is always given an opportunity to explain any situations in his past which might require modification of the wording of the questions.

For instance, a standard pre-employment type question might be, "Have you ever been convicted of a crime?" The subject might say that at the age of nineteen he had been arrested for petty shoplifting and pleaded guilty. If this is the case, then the original question could not possibly be used and would require a rewording. The pre-test interview is absolutely essential, and a review of the questions to be utilized in the examination must be made, giving the examinee the opportunity to make explanations so that proper rewording can be accomplished.

The Examination

The actual polygraph examination consists of two or more tests. Each would typically consist of ten or twelve questions (in the case of wrist-type blood pressure cuff, as many as twenty questions might be asked). Each test consumes about three to four minutes. Irrelevant questions are normally interspersed with relevant questions and also at one or two strategic points in the examination the control questions are asked. Irrelevant questions are intended to be completely neutral to the examinee—questions such as, "Is this the month of February?", "Is your first name John?", "Is your last name Smith?", "Are you wearing a tie?", "Are you in New York City at the present time?", etc.

Relevant areas of inquiry in a pre-employment examination are selected by the client and usually fall within the following scope: deliberate falsification of application; deliberate falsification of medical history; illicit use of dangerous drugs or narcotics; thefts of cash from former employers; theft of merchandise from former employers; being discharged, or forced to resign from a previous job; significant trouble while in the military; serious unsolved criminal offenses; criminal complaints and convictions; and in the case of a recently hired employee working on a probationary status, thefts from the present employer since employment.

Because polygraph questions must be answered with a simple "yes" or "no," it is quite common that a person undergoing an examination will think of some situation which may or may not be directly relevant to the issue, but which is triggered in the thought process by a particular question. Such thought processes will usually reflect themselves in the polygraph tracing and can easily be discussed with the examiner at the conclusion of each run.

Normally, at the end of the first run the polygraphist will give the examinee an opportunity to volunteer any information that may have come to mind during the actual run. If nothing is volunteered at that point, the polygraphist will proceed to administer the second run, after which the polygraphist will discuss in detail the polygram or chart with the subject and pointedly inquire as to anything that may have come into the subject's mind in relation to any particular question which produced a response. Any explanation on the part of the subject will simply require further rephrasing or rewording of the question, something along the lines of, "Other than what you have told me, have you _____?"

Should a subject resort to outright deception, the examiner will discuss it in a frank and candid manner and afford the subject the opportunity to explain the true facts in the area at issue. If an explanation is offered, then the examiner will run one further chart, commonly called a "clearing chart."

Propriety of Questions

Ethical standards in the polygraph field require the examiner to be very strict in assuring the propriety of questions used. Most examiners will resist the rare attempt by an employer to check areas which are not relevant to the job sought by the applicant. Obviously, each examination is different because of the age and background of the subject, and the nature of the job for which he is applying.

A rule-of-thumb approach to the propriety of questions would follow approximately these lines:

- A 35-year-old applicant for a supermarket manager's job would in all probability not be questioned about boyhood thefts or even thefts from employers at an early age, especially if the applicant has held positions which afforded him access to money and merchandise and where it can be determined that he has refrained from such thefts during the past ten years.

- On the other hand, an 18-year-old applicant for a position involving the handling of merchandise or cash, could properly be questioned as to thefts committed within the past several years.

- A 17-year-old girl applying for a position as a drugstore clerk would probably not be questioned regarding chronic and expensive use of alcohol but she might very well be asked about illicit drug use.

- A 30-year-old applicant for a job as an airline pilot would not be questioned regarding his being fired from prior jobs as a teenager but could very well be asked a question concerning chronic and excessive use of alcohol.

In summary, then, it is evident that in order to be of real service to his client and the examinee, the polygraphist must use only questions which have some definite bearing on the applicant's fitness for the job. Unless a person is applying for a job so sensitive in nature as to raise the question of possible blackmail, there is no reason for the polygraphist to delve into such highly personal areas as sexual relations or sexual deviation. In the typical pre-employment situation involving commercial business firms, questions of this type are never asked during either the pre-test interview or the test itself.

Chapter 19

SO YOU WANT TO BEAT THE POLYGRAPH!

By Carl S. Klump

When people ask my profession and are told I am a lie-detector examiner (or, as we prefer to call it, a polygraph examiner), one of the first questions that follows is, "Does that thing really work?" My own father asked me that when I first entered the profession.

The proper answer to the question is, of course, "Yes, it does work, but only in the hands of a person who knows how to use it." Public opinion seems to be that the instrument is capable of determining, all by itself, whether or not a person is telling a lie.

Let me say that a polygraph instrument is just that: an instrument. It is designed to record on chart paper certain physiological information put into it by the person taking the test. A qualified examiner must interpret the marks left on the paper, and it is this interpretation that helps the examiner form an opinion of truth or untruth. Without a qualified examiner, the instrument has little value.

When I speak of professional examiners, I mean to exclude both the inexperienced examiner with little training and less supervision, and the professional interrogator who uses the test mainly as a

© 1965, 1975, Security World Publishing Co., Inc.

"gimmick" around which to build an aggressive interrogation. The professional examiner, I feel, is one who, by reason of his education, extensive and advanced training (numbered in years, not months), research, and contribution to the field, is prepared to treat the polygraph examination as a diagnostic technique. A qualified examiner, in my opinion, is one who need not lean on interrogation to determine truthfulness or deception, but one who can find his answer, efficiently, in the polygraph records alone, because the examination has been properly conducted.

My own standard for examiner-trainees includes a degree in criminology, police science, police administration, or another related but acceptable field. The professional examiner needs to be well versed in abnormalities of physiology and psychology, particularly in terms of their effect on the test. The trainee is expected to work under complete supervision for a year, and to attend a local college for those courses in which he may be deficient. The trainee must learn that his duty is not to seek a lie; he must first seek the truth. And when the examiner-trainee has finished his "intern" year of training, he is expected to be aware that his professional status has not yet begun and will not begin until he has made significant contributions to the field.

Polygraph No Mystery

There is no mystery about the instrument. Almost all polygraphs work the same way and have at least three pens: one for blood pressure and pulse; one for respiration; and the third for galvanic skin response. Some polygraphs have additional pens for specialized purposes such as muscular tension or blood flow.

I am amused by people who tell me they are electronics experts and have devised a "foolproof" method of beating the lie detector. It seems to do little good to tell them that knowledge of electronics will not help them because the instrument functions pneumatically, as well as electronically. It does not seem to occur to them that, even should they be able to alter one or more of the factors tested, their chances of duplicating a genuinely truthful test by those means is, so far as any examiner knows, almost impossible. When a person tries to cheat on a test, the chances are that it will be spotted. But a lot of people try it.

A very important criterion in determining deception, in fact, is whether the subject does attempt to "beat" the test. Although it is possible to completely distort polygraph records to the point where they can no longer be interpreted question for question, the person who does so is informing the examiner that he is seeking to conceal his reaction to one or more questions to "beat the examiner."

"Faking" High Blood Pressure

Some time ago a man came in for a test as a result of an anonymous phone call to his boss, the owner of a small grocery store. The caller said the employee was stealing merchandise out of the back door. Sam, the employee, was informed of the call by his employer. He was most indignant, as any innocent person might well be, and he suggested to the employer that he be allowed to take a "lie-detector" test to prove his innocence. He even offered to pay for the test himself.

When he came in for his appointment he again expressed his indignation. Although he offered his complete cooperation, he said he was bothered by bursitis in both shoulders and couldn't raise his arms. As he sat in the examining chair, it became obvious he was holding something hidden beneath his arms. He was allowed to keep his secret and the test was eventually completed. The polygraph records revealed quite significant deception when he denied stealing from the store and, when Sam was told of the result, he became vituperative and abusive.

After he cooled down a bit, I told him that perhaps the items he was holding under his arms were not helping him defeat the test and I invited him to remove them. All his indignation vanished as he took two cakes of soap from under his arms. At that point there was no stopping him from telling about the merchandise he had been stealing from the store.

As to why he secreted the soap under his arms, he told me, "A couple of years ago I got a call for the draft and I didn't want to go. A friend told me to rub soap under my arms and I would get high blood pressure. I figured if it worked for the army, it should work for the lie detector. I guess it didn't."

It was suggested to him that perhaps the soap did not really create high blood pressure; that he might have had it all along. About a week later he called to inform me that he had seen a physician and was under treatment for high blood pressure.

Counter-irritants Don't Work

People are continually hiding things on their persons in an effort to beat the test. One lady, a cashier in a discount store who was taking a routine test (she was required to take a test every six months) told me after she failed her test that she had put some very coarse sandpaper in her girdle. She thought she would be so aggravated at the sandpaper that nothing could show up on her test.

Then there was Jack, sent in for a test by a judge to see if he had stolen his friend's social security check. Jack claimed he was so hard of hearing that I had to shout at him. The louder I shouted, the louder his answers became. This seemed peculiar, so I purposely bumped his foot a bit and said lightly, "Oh, excuse me!" Jack assured me "That's all right." Then I called the judge to find out just how hard of hearing Jack really was. The judge said Jack had heard him all right in the courtroom. Jack never told me what he hoped to gain by feigning deafness, but I assume he wanted me to think he was so deaf he couldn't be tested. In view of the fact that deaf mutes have been successfully tested, that would seem a faint hope.

Drinking Won't Do It

Another favorite trick is to stop by the washroom to drink a quantity of some alcoholic beverage immediately before the test. Vodka seems to be preferred, judging by the empty bottles I find in the washroom. Apparently these people think it can't be smelled on their breath.

What happens is this: Harry comes in after his trip to the washroom bar, ready to take his test and prepared to beat it because he has just finished off a half-pint. As time wears on—the test actually takes upward of an hour—Harry's fortification begins to take effect. He becomes sleepy and wiggly; his speech becomes slurred—Harry is getting drunk before my eyes and beginning to smell like an accident at a distillery.

Before he gets drunk enough to have any real effect on the test, it is over. By now, however, he is talkative, and it is a simple matter to lead his conversation to his misdeeds, whatever they may have been.

I remember one man who tried this method. John was a head cashier in a bank, and was ordinarily a non-drinker. After he failed his test, he became very talkative and told me of his defalcations, all very readily, and laughing all the time. Since he was too unsteady to write out a confession, it was decided to let him tell his story to another witness. As John stood up to shake hands with the witness, his knees buckled and he dropped to the floor. His story was re-told on his knees amid much laughter, after which he just lay down on the floor and slept. We checked his story with the bank, just in case, but it checked out just as he had related it.

Breathing Oddly Has Been Tried

Another favorite trick is to run around the building before coming in for the test. Some have even run up the eleven flights of stairs, appearing at the laboratory very flustered and very much out of breath. The only thing facing these people is a wait in the waiting room while they get their breath back.

Some time ago, an individual wrote a letter to a newspaper which was printed in the "Letters to the Editor" column. The letter explained an easy method of beating the test by "holding your breath when the question is asked; then, when you answer, just breathe very rapidly." Throughout the next week, subjects with something to hide were alternately holding their breath and breathing rapidly.

About three years ago Joe, a janitor, almost beat me on the test. Joe's employer called to set up an appointment and explained about five different thefts of money from tenants' apartments. He didn't like to suspect Joe, but the janitor had been seen near all five of the apartments before the thefts were discovered. When Joe appeared for his test, he brought a letter from the manager stating that the police had solved three of the thefts and would I confine the test to the remaining two unsolved thefts. Joe passed his test, indicating he hadn't stolen the two amounts of money, but there was something unexplainable wrong with the polygraph records; they just didn't look right. He was asked about this but could offer no suggestion as to what might be wrong.

After Joe left the laboratory, I received a call from his lawyer, who attempted to explain the subject's physical condition as a possible cause for the records having looked so peculiar. The lawyer talked no more like a lawyer than would have a tugboat captain. This, of course, compounded the original suspicion that something was wrong and a call was made to Joe's employer. It was then that I found the letter cancelling the three "solved" thefts was not written by the employer, nor had the three thefts been solved.

Joe was brought back for another test covering the remaining three thefts. This time he failed the test and subsequently admitted stealing the money. He also told me that the "lawyer" was his brother-in-law, who had stolen the money in the other two thefts covered by Joe's first test.

Tranquilizers No Solution

Tranquilizers were popular not long ago as a means to beat the test. One group of examinees sought an attorney to guide them. If they had to do it over again, they would probably pick another attorney; he had advised them to take tranquilizers before the tests. In they came for their examinations, confident the tranquilizers would cause the tests to show their "innocence." But the lawyer forgot one important thing: while a tranquilizer calms a person down, it usually has little effect on those physiological functions of the body which we measure. Each person sat there calm and collected while the tranquilizers removed the ordinary nervousness found in any person faced with a polygraph test. Consequently, their tests were remarkably evident, showing nicely where they lied.

Almost every person has his own method of trying to outwit the machine. Some answer "yes" under their breath and say "no" out loud. That doesn't work. Some say they just don't remember and refuse to answer yes or no. That doesn't work either, because the question is merely changed to "Do you remember doing such and such?"

How do you "beat a lie detector"? The answer is very simple: be stupid. Ignorant, uneducated people who are not even trying to beat the test, who don't even care about the outcome, are very often difficult to detect in their lies.

Contrary to what most people think, the more intelligent a person is, the more difficult it will be for him to actually beat the test.

The Mystery of the "Perfect" Test

Dick had a master's degree in psychology and was suspected of trying to murder his wife. His story made several policemen's eyebrows rise, and he was requested to take a polygraph test.

Dick's records from his test were remarkably clear. They were absolutely consistent and without a single variation; they were too perfect. Dick's records revealed each and every breath the exact same size. There was not the slightest variation in either the height of amplitude or in the rate of breathing. (I have attempted to approximate this type of record by attaching myself to the instrument, but could do so only while watching the pen move; Dick was looking straight ahead.)

What makes his records so peculiar is that the normal tendency to suppress when asked a question is absent. Since his test contained a control question, "Did you ever purposely hurt anyone?", a question quite mild and very wide in time and scope, and there was no emotional response evident at this question, it became apparent that he was purposely "controlling" his respiration.

Compare, for example, the emotional impact of this control question to the relevant question, "Did you hit your wife on the head with that kitchen stool?" If he were innocent of the attempted murder, his attention would be drawn to the question about purposely hurting someone, since no one is capable of passing this wide a question without some explanation. A guilty person, however, could care less about the "hurt" question; he wants only not to be found out on the "hit on the head" question.

So a control question test boils down to an emotional response appearing somewhere in the test. If it appears to the control question, there is a tendency toward a lie to the relevant question. Nowhere did Dick show an emotional response.

Is A False "Untruthful" Possible?

There are many things that can cause foreign reactions to occur in an examination. For example, a truly angry person may produce a chart comparable to that produced by a subject who is untruthful.

Occasionally a person will be innocent of the specific issue about which he is being tested, yet may be guilty of another, unrelated (but perhaps similar) event. Ordinarily this does not affect the examination, but it can. In a case where eight men were examined for knowledge of a theft of money from a market, one showed certain knowledge and two others had to be re-examined because of "general disturbances" throughout their polygraph records. When brought to the laboratory, we were able to "read through" the peculiar disturbances and clear them of the theft under question. Later I learned what the disturbances had meant: they had been involved in other thefts from the store.

They'll Try Anything

But the smartest attempt to beat the test I've ever seen made me feel a little foolish. A mousy little fellow being tested on narcotics peddling for a suburban police department thought up this one. During the original checkout of the instrument as attached to him, his responses were coming through just fine; but as soon as the questions were asked, the blood pressure pen would stop and leave only a straight line. Try as I might, I couldn't find what was causing it.

Finally I noticed the subject make a small movement just as the pen stopped moving. The test was stopped and started over again. This time, however, I was looking for that little movement. Sure enough, there it was, just as the pen stopped moving.

I'll never know where he got his idea from because he refused to complete the test after I found out what he was doing. He was stepping on the hose from his blood-pressure cuff, leading to the instrument. By pinching it shut, none of his responses could get through to the instrument.

There is an important lesson to be learned from the various ways people try to beat a lie-detector test, or—more accurately— the examiner. It is easier to "beat" an inexperienced or careless examiner; indeed, I know of a firm with a reputation of passing everyone they test. It is not so easy to "beat" the professional examiner. Actually, the professional examiner surreptitiously invites the subject to try to beat the test, if the examinee is so inclined, knowing that the attempt itself can be informative.

My advice is this: a person who has something to lie about, shouldn't take the test. He who tries to beat the test, only makes my job easier.

(Editor's Note: The following is a letter sent by Mr. Klump's polygraph firm to those private businesses who desire to initiate a polygraph testing program.)

Suggested Policy When Initiating Polygraph Examinations of Employees

Experience has shown that approximately fifty percent of any given group of employees have stolen goods or merchandise from places of employment where adequate controls were not prevalent. The majority of these thefts can be considered individually minor, but when viewed in their totality, these thefts gain major importance.

Polygraph examinations are seldom accepted by an employee who has nothing to gain from the conducting of such examinations. The employee who has stolen expects only to lose. He tends not only to refuse the examination, but entices others to refuse the tests. Refusal to be examined, alone, is never sufficient grounds to warrant a conclusion of deception, since ordinary, honest employees may refuse the tests for reasons of their own.

The modern employer who desires to "find out who has been stealing in the past" usually finds the majority of his employees refusing to accept a program of periodic polygraph examinations. Such refusal may even lead to complaints being made to a union, whether or not the employees are unionized. Several unions prevent all polygraph examinations under any circumstances; some unions sanction the examinations if certain conditions are met. Acceptance of such a program by a union is often predicated on the answer to the question: Will our union members get a fair shake?

The type of periodic screening polygraph examination which is most often accepted by unions (if any is accepted at all) is the examination following an "Amnesty Date." An Amnesty Date is a date at which time all employees are informed that polygraph examinations are scheduled for some future date and that the questions appearing in the examination will deal with the employee's integrity with the company since the date of announcement. The employee is expressly made to understand that no questions will be asked about the employee's possible acts of dishonesty which may have occurred before the announcement.

The motive for an Amnesty Date is clear: All employees, even those who have been pilfering in the past, have nothing to lose by accepting the program. There are few valid reasons remaining for anyone to refuse the program.

In announcing the inception of a polygraph program, the employer should discuss it with each employee individually. The employer should explain the real, actual reason for the necessity of the program. The employer should never resort to make-believe excuses for starting the program. If there has been an abnormal inventory loss, it should be explained as such. If visual or other observations have proved pilferage, it should be explained as such.

The following announcement should be reprinted on company stationery and posted, after discussing the program with the employees, for employee reading:

"John H. Jones & Company has been engaging in several discussions with our insurance company as a result of our claim regarding several acts of dishonesty which occurred recently. We are informed by our insurance representative that a polygraph screening program may lead to a reduction (rather than an increase, as is now the case) in our insurance premiums, provided all Jones & Company employees cooperate.

"In order to protect the fidelity and dignity of our employees, we have contacted one of the leading polygraph examiners in the country, Mr. Carl S. Klump. Mr. Klump, who holds a degree in Criminology, is dedicated to fair and impartial examinations. He had advised us that such a program will be initiated for Jones & Company provided the following conditions are met:

1. No person will be examined against his will.
2. Every employee will be given equal opportunity.
3. Employees are to be informed of impending examinations prior to the examination. Surprise examinations are not tolerated.
4. Each person shall be informed as of a certain date that he is held responsible for his integrity after the date of announcement only. He will not be examined about his integrity with the company before that time of notice.
5. No personal questions are to be requested or asked during the examination.
6. Questions during the examination will concern themselves with integrity (since the date of announcement)

and necessary questions of an irrelevant and control nature only.

7. The report of the examination is to be made confidential to Mr. John Jones only.
8. Each employee examined shall be informed by the examiner as to the results of his own examination immediately following the test.

"Although the dishonest actions of a few have necessitated this program, we are assured of the integrity possessed by the large majority of our co-workers. We are also assured that our employees readily accept this new program and will cooperate in assistance in the reduction of our overhead by reducing insurance rates."

The first examinations following the posting of the notice should be scheduled three months in advance. Succeeding examinations should be conducted at no less than six months nor more than one year intervals.

New employees should be given a pre-employment screening examination before being hired. New employees, having successfully passed a screening examination, can be re-examined in six months.

In those cases where a specific item is missing at a specific time, those individuals who had ready access to the missing item may be asked about their knowledge of the event and may be asked to submit to a polygraph examination concerning their answers. It is not proper to request the examiner to find out other items of information not having a relationship with the missing item.

The above policy has been utilized by this laboratory since its inauguration. To date, there has been no complaint made to any union by any employee regarding the polygraph program when conducted as above stated.

Carl S. Klump

President of Chicago Professional Polygraph Center, Inc., Mr. Klump graduated from the School of Criminology at the University of California at Berkeley. He served eight years in military intelligence and military police.

Mr. Klump developed the Stanton Pre-employment Survey, a written test used to determine honesty/dishonesty attitudes in job applicants. Among his published articles in the field of polygraphy are "Arriving at a Control Question in Criminal Cases," "Principles of Controlled Stimulation," "Your Rights When Asked to Take a Lie Detector Test" and "Morality and the Lie Detector."

Section Three:
DETERRING
INTERNAL THEFT

VII.
PRE-EMPLOYMENT
SCREENING

Chapter 20

PRE-EMPLOYMENT BACKGROUND INVESTIGATIONS

By D. L. Wood

An old proverb suggests that you can't make racehorses out of plow horses—and vice versa. The truth of this adage applies with special force in the area of employment. Background investigation—designed to do much more than separate the fleet racer from the dray—can save companies a tremendous amount of money. It is undeniable that no organization is better than the people it brings into its unit.

There are a number of situations in which background investigations become very important. The first is when new employees are brought into an organization. The second, probably equally important, is when promotions are to be made, either from within or, more importantly, from outside the organization.

A recent case illustrates how important background investigation can be. A firm was about to bring in a new executive for a very sensitive, specialized position. Fortunately, the company's security department was asked to check the man's background prior to the appointment. It was a rather tricky investigation, because the man

From a presentation given at the International Security Conference in Chicago, 1970.

held a very high position at that time. A few phone calls were made to well-placed individuals, and it was determined that this man was beyond doubt a very intelligent, well-informed individual in his field. The investigation also found, however, that he was a non-conformist. He might work on a project for 36 hours straight, then disappear for the next few days. He was very adverse to any kind of supervision.

Another check discovered that this man had been arrested for disorderly conduct. A further check disclosed he had also been arrested as a suspected burglar. Although he had never been convicted, he had been found on the roof of a major store building with burglar tools.

When these facts were brought to management's attention, they decided that they did not have a place in their organization for this kind of man. The company would have been buying trouble. It is almost impossible to say how much it might have cost the company if the investigation had not been conducted.

Background investigations become more and more important each day, particularly in large organizations where there is strong labor control. In most organizations there is a probationary period for new employees of 30, 60, or 90 days. Ordinarily the employer does not have to state its reasons for relieving an employee of his responsibilities during that period of time. After the probationary period is over, however, usually a formal hearing will be required. Obviously, it is highly advisable to complete a background investigation during the probationary period.

Importance of Application Form

The employment application can be very important in supplying information needed by the investigator. The security department should have good liaison with the personnel department, labor relations department, or whoever handles the matter of bringing prospective employees in and getting the applications. Security should specify what information is needed to make the application more complete and helpful to the background investigator.

In addition to asking for the applicant's name, the application should ask, "Have you ever used any other name?" It makes a great difference to the course of investigation if all names that this person has used are not known. A man who at one time had a long name, for example, may have shortened it to something very similar. It will save the investigator a lot of time and work if he can be sure he knows the correct name and any other names the applicant has used.

The application should ask not only for the applicant's present address, but for a list of his residences for the past ten years, in chronological order. The present residence, of course, is important to the investigator; he will begin his investigation there and go on back through his full residency period. If possible, all telephone numbers the applicant has had during the last ten years should be included as well. If there is not time or manpower available to personally contact all places of residence, a short-cut may be taken by using telephone numbers. Phone numbers may reveal, in addition, whether the applicant has listed phony addresses.

Value of Pre-Employment Agreements

The issue of privacy is another reason why liaison between the investigator and the personnel or labor relations department is important. It is becoming more and more difficult today to obtain information on the private lives of people, which is what a background investigation amounts to. Charges of invasion of privacy arise in many cases.

It is an investigator's job to find out everything he possibly can about the individual he is investigating. With the help of the personnel or labor relations department, a number of pre-employment agreements can be made which will assist the background investigator in his task.

For example, prospective employees may be asked to sign a statement agreeing to take polygraph examinations at the employer's request. Such a statement might read: "I fully understand and agree that as a condition of my employment at _____ , I will submit to a polygraph (lie detector) examination should I be selected on a departmental random basis, or at any time if requested by the company. I further understand and agree that _____ reserves the right to determine the continuation or termination of my employment in the light of the results of said polygraph (lie detector) examination." (This particular agreement is, of course, subject to applicable state laws restricting polygraph use.)

New employees may also be required to fill out a bonding form.

This is a good psychological deterrent to the applicant, who realizes that if he absconds with company funds, he will be turned over to the bonding company for restitution. In addition, there are a number of things on the bonding form which give the investigator further insight into the applicant.

It is a good idea to have the applicant give written permission for the employer to contact various agencies in checking his background. These include: 1) police departments in towns where he has lived or been employed; 2) schools he has attended; 3) past employers; 4) credit companies; 5) insurance companies; 6) military branches.

This written permission can be most important. It is becoming increasingly difficult for the security investigator to check criminal records. Some school officials are very sensitive about giving out information on former students. If the investigator can show signed permission from the applicant, however, he has one foot in the door. The same is true so far as past employers, credit companies, insurance companies, and the military are concerned.

Documents Required from Applicant

The applicant should be required to present certain documents as a condition of employment. These include his birth certificate, military papers, diplomas from any institution from which he has graduated. If the job requires a high school education, he should be required to present his high school diploma or GED. If the applicant must have a license to operate some type of machinery, he should present a certificate showing he is qualified to do so.

An investigation may be avoided entirely if the personnel department has established a clear job description listing the requirements for a particular job. If the applicant does not meet all requirements for age, height, weight, education, bondability, etc., no investigation need be made. Especially when investigatory manpower is short, it is important to avoid unnecessary investigations.

A Working Outline

With these conditions of employment established, the investigator is in a good position to begin his background check on the applicant. The following is an outline of items that should be included in a good background investigation.

1)   Name and Aliases

As already mentioned, this is where the investigation must begin. If the investigator has the wrong name, he will waste a lot of time.

2)   Necessary Papers

These include a birth certificate. People born prior to around 1910 may have a hard time locating their birth certificates. Other documents may be accepted in lieu of a birth certificate. Baptismal certificates will stand in good stead, as well as an affidavit from one of the parents. Citizenship papers or records of the individual's early school attendance will also serve as good birth records. Military papers may not be entirely reliable as a record of birth, since people sometimes lie about their age to get into the service.

Citizenship papers should be required, if the applicant is not a natural-born citizen.

Military papers should be required. In addition to his discharge papers, the applicant should bring his DD-214 form (notice of separation), which gives a record of when the individual entered the service, where he served, how he served, any awards, any disciplinary action that may have been held against him. It also shows any prior service he may have had. Discharges include "honorable," "dishonorable," and "under honorable conditions." The category "under honorable conditions" can cover many things, some of them not very creditable to the individual. This should be checked.

3)   Residences

Using the chronological list of residences obtained in the employment application, the investigator must verify that these are the places where the person has actually lived. He should knock on doors and ask, "Did John Doe live here at this particular time?"

The verification of residency may be combined with a neighborhood investigation. The investigator must approach the neighborhood investigation with the thought that he is going to find out everything about the applicant—not only the good, but the bad as well. When neighbors are interviewed, they are more likely than not to say, "Oh, he's a fine man." They don't want to say anything bad. This must be overcome by questions like, "We know that everyone has weaknesses. What are this man's weaknesses? Does he drink? How long has he lived here? How does he get along with his neighbors? Does he fight with his wife? Does he pay his bills? Is he the kind of man that you like as a neighbor? What time does he come home at night? What kind of a car does he drive? What is his appearance?"

The investigator should also go to the local tavern or grocery store and ask the personnel, "What do you know about John Doe?" A bartender may not be too willing to discuss a good customer. The investigator must do a good job of selling, to convince the tavern-keeper that he is there to find out everything about the applicant, who will be in a position of trust.

An unannounced home interview of the applicant is important in any investigation, especially for applicants for jobs in the security department. The condition of the man's home may tell a great deal about him. If there is evidence of excessive drinking, for example, it may be he is not the kind of person the company wants to employ. The general look of his home, the appearance of his wife and children, tell a lot about him, perhaps more than can be learned in any other way.

In the case of an applicant for a security position, it is important that the investigator talk to his wife. He may have to work nights. How does his wife feel about her husband's working from midnight to nine a.m.? If she doesn't like this, chances are the employee will not be very happy and will not stay on the job long. If the wife does not take a positive attitude toward security or law enforcement, or if she refuses to talk to the investigator altogether, this may also indicate possible trouble.

4)   Criminal Records

While law enforcement officers have access to criminal records, it is difficult for private security officers to check an applicant's background for criminal activity. If possible, however, criminal records should be checked on the following types of employees: security personnel; cashiers, or anyone who will be handling money; promotions to executive positions. (Many people manage to move up through the ranks of organizations despite criminal backgrounds.)

Employees of the security force may be checked by being asked to obtain special police commissions. To obtain such a commission, the applicant must be fingerprinted and his prints cleared through the police department.

Some companies require every applicant to be fingerprinted. This serves a psychological purpose. Learning they must be fingerprinted, many prospective applicants walk out. Others start to work, but disappear after their first paycheck. The con knows approximately how long it takes to get his prints classified and back, and by that time, he's gone. He may have taken some of the company's property with him, but he has been eliminated from employment.

Another advantage of fingerprinting employees occurs if print comparisons on latent prints are needed in any later investigation.

Civil actions are also important. Has a man gone through bankruptcy? If he cannot handle his own money, chances are he is not going to handle the employer's money any better. Has he been involved in lawsuits against his prior employers? Has he had personal injury suits against them? This is very important today, when some employees seem to have the attitude, "I'm going to get every buck I can from my employer."

Has the applicant's driver's license ever been revoked? Has it been revoked more than once? This is particularly important, of course, if the prospective job requires driving.

5) Membership in Organizations

What organizations does the applicant belong to? Are any of them listed as subversive by the Attorney General's office?

In investigating for an executive position, the applicant's memberships in social clubs may indicate the type of people he associates with.

6) School Records

The investigator should learn the dates and places of school attendance, grades and degrees obtained, and whether the individual has a GED.

Too often investigators try to check school records by telephone. Very often school authorities will not give out any information over the telephone. Someone must go in person to talk to the school authorities in order to obtain proper school records. Very often an applicant will claim that he graduated from a certain institution; when the investigator checks, he may find the applicant attended for a time but did not graduate.

7) Employment

The application should include a ten-year chronological list of the places where the applicant has been employed. The investigator must verify this list. The only way this can be done is by personal contact with previous employers. If an investigator calls a past employer on the phone and says, "We're thinking of hiring John Doe," chances are the employer will reply, "Oh, he's a fine man." "Would you rehire him?" "Oh, yes."

If, however, the investigator goes to talk to the employer face to face, he may learn the applicant resigned, possibly because of absenteeism, or because he couldn't pay his debts, or he had a drinking problem. . .any number of reasons.

The investigator should be alert for any lapses in the chronological data given by the applicant. If the applicant has stated that he was self-employed for a period of time, the investigator should be aware that the term "self-employment" may cover a multitude of sins. He may have been in jail or in a mental institution during the time he says he was self-employed. The investigator should give careful and close attention to any period of "self-employment."

8) Social Status

Is the applicant married? Has he been married? Is he presently divorced or separated? Does he have dependents, either children or other members of the family?

9) Physical Condition

The applicant's general appearance, of course, is an indication of his health. He should be required to undergo a medical examination. In addition, the neighborhood investigation mentioned earlier may give an indication of the applicant's physical condition. Does he take part in any sports activities?

10) Debts

The employment application should ask for information about the applicant's debts. The investigator should try to determine whether he has listed all of his debts, and whether he is paying those people he does owe money to. There are various centralized sources of credit information in various cities.

Finally, after all background information has been gathered, the investigator must analyze it. His summary statement should include any derogatory items he has uncovered in his investigation. His report will include his conclusions and recommendations. In his opinion, is this the kind of man that should be hired for this particular job?

D.L. Wood

Mr. Wood served as a Special Agent with the FBI from 1940 until 1947, when he joined Illinois Central Railroad as Chief Special Agent and Director of Special Services.

He left Illinois Central in 1970 to become Director of Security for Carson, Pirie, Scott and Company in Chicago. In 1972–1973, Mr. Wood served as a consultant on a team of six specialists furnished by Burns International Security Services, Inc., for a loss prevention survey of Amtrak. Since May of 1973 he has been manager of investigations for Shannon Consultants in St. Paul, Minn.

Mr. Wood has been a member of the Society of Former Special Agents of the FBI and the International Association of Chiefs of Police. He is a past president of the Protective Section, Association of American Railroads; Special Agents Association of Chicago; and the Chicago Railroad Special Agents and Police Association. He holds a B.A. from Macalester College and an LL.B. from St. Paul College of Law.

Chapter 21

BACKGROUND INVESTIGATION:
WELL WORTH THE COST

By John S. Alden

Why conduct a background investigation? Very basically, the answer is: to establish that what an individual says and puts down about his background in an employment application is true; that he is what he represents himself to be.

When your company hires a new employee, do they really know with whom they are dealing?

For example, a gentleman sold himself to a personnel department as a physicist with a Ph.D. He knew from experience that it would be at least six months before the company discovered his deception. They hired him at $35,000 a year. For six months they kept him in a pool doing nothing. At the end of six months, they realized he was not qualified for the job and fired him. He had already collected half of his $35,000 salary. He had a history of doing this at many companies. If they had taken the time to check his background to make sure that what he said was true, they would have saved themselves some money.

In another case, I received a request to do a quick background

From a presentation given at the International Security Conference in Los Angeles, 1971.

check on an applicant for a research position. I called a friend to inquire about the applicant and he replied, "That's very strange . . . the man you're asking about is sitting in my office right now." The applicant had borrowed the entire background and bona fides of the man he was representing himself to be.

Large and small companies alike are taken in by such deception. In our changing society people move constantly. The employer can no longer take the individual at face value, particularly when money is involved.

In another unfortunate case, a company decided to save money by doing its own background check on a prospective controller instead of hiring an investigative agency. They checked the applicant's references by telephone and received glowing reports. He was hired, and everything was fine. . .until one day he did not show up, and neither did $30,000. It was later discovered that the address he had given was a vacant lot. The references were either his own telephone number of those of his buddies. If the company had spent a couple of hundred dollars to check the man, they would have bought "insurance" to save $30,000.

What method of selecting new employees can prevent such occurrences? Many companies use initial personal interviews and psychological tests. These are very valuable aids, but they do not give a complete answer. In fact, biographical background investigations are not the complete answer. Human beings are, we all know, complex; background investigation is a very inexact science. There is no way to be 100% effective; but we need to use every tool at our command to try to determine all we possibly can.

Many companies have elaborate security systems, yet at closing time they leave the premises to a contract janitorial service. Often the executive responsible for the company's security does not know anything about these people who will be entering the premises after hours. Often he does not even know whether the contract service has done any background checks on its employees. Too often the company becomes aware of this security vulnerability only after a loss occurs.

We tend to think sometimes of security or protection in terms of devices. . .alarms, locks, CCTV, etc. We fail to recognize that people are really where security begins. In many companies the presidents, executive vice presidents, managers, etc., are hired by word-of-mouth recommendation alone. Background investigation is never considered, until suddenly the company finds that perhaps it has made a rather expensive mistake.

The best way to sell management on the need for background investigation is by emphasizing that the company will save money in the long run. By investing "X" dollars in background checks, they are buying "insurance" against hiring employees who will cause loss. In addition, the information obtained in background investigations will be a tool that management can use to its advantage, not only in placement of new employees, but in promotions and in using personnel to the most economical advantage possible.

Cost Factors

The cost of a background investigation will vary with the type of coverage desired and the time required for completion. Is the information needed in five days, ten days, or thirty days? The quicker it is required, the more the investigation will cost.

The depth of coverage desired will depend on the position involved. Will the investigation go back five years into the individual's background, or ten, or fifteen years? Within those time periods, what points will be covered?

What geographical areas will the investigation cover? Have the individual's activities been confined to a local area, or has he moved across the country? The more areas that must be checked, the more it will cost.

An investigation into an individual's background for the past five years, including his employments, present or most significant neighborhood, financial background, criminal record if available (by law, an investigative agency can report only that which is public record) will cost $60 to $130. A ten-year investigation covering the same points would run probably in the neighborhood of $150 to $200. Again, this will depend on the time required for completion and the specific coverage desired. An average fifteen-year check would run $200 to $350.

If the position involves a $25,000 or $35,000 annual salary, a background check is really rather cheap insurance. In view of this, can a company really afford not to check a person? In my opinion, it cannot. And yet often security or personnel procedures are considered part of overhead expense. When times get rough and the budget must be cut, the first thing to be cut is overhead. . .including security. Does this really save money?

I've heard many a professional security officer say he would love to have a job where the only salary he would receive would be a nice percentage of what he saves the company.

Outside vs. Inside Investigators

When instituting background investigations of personnel, a company must decide whether to hire its own personnel to conduct investigations, or use the services of an outside agency. There are pros and cons to both approaches. An outside company will perhaps be more impartial than a man on the firm's own staff. By the same token, the staff investigator is probably better known to and trusted by management.

Beginning the Investigation

How does a company decide which positions should have background checks? This will depend on the duties of the position, what the employee will be exposed to, what he will be entrusted with. In some cases it may be more important to check the shipping clerk than the office manager.

A background investigation should begin with the Personal History Statement (PHS). At this point the personnel officer usually has an opportunity to sit down with the applicant, discuss his background with him, and make sure that the application is filled out completely and legibly. All questions should be answered; those that do not apply should be filled in "NA."

With increasing charges of "invasion of privacy" today, it is advisable to inform the applicant that all items he has put down on his application will be verified, and to obtain a written statement from him allowing the employer's authorized agent to have access to educational, employment, and other records. Without this written consent, particularly in educational institutions, the information may not be made available to the investigator.

Management must decide what depth and degree of coverage they want, again related to cost. How much are they willing to spend? What do they want to know? Do they want to verify everything on the application, or merely certain things? Are they interested in the applicant's suitability for the job, or just in verifying what he says?

Assuming that management does want to verify what the applicant has said on his application, the minimum coverage should include at least his last employment and his present neighborhood (which would include contacting neighbors). In addition to this, his financial background should probably be covered, to be sure he is not deeply in debt. Criminal records should be checked, if possible. If the position involves driving, his driving record should be checked. If he will be operating a company vehicle or machinery, his insurability is important.

Management must also decide how soon the information is needed. When a union is involved, there is usually a probationary period before an employee becomes permanent. This will enter into the decision on timing. How soon a new employee is needed will also affect this decision, as will the state of the labor market. If a new employee is needed immediately, and there is a shortage of qualified people available, it will not be practical to wait 30 days to perform a background check.

Details of Full Investigation

In a full background investigation on someone who will be in a responsible position, going back at least 15 years, or perhaps to birth, what things should be covered?

Date and place of birth should be verified. The applicant's educational background should be checked. Did he graduate from where he said he did? Is he qualified in the field he says he is? His past employment record should be examined. This should go beyond a simple check of personnel records. Often the personnel record is simply a card stating that so-and-so was employed from such-and-such a date to such-and-such a date, and is eligible for re-hire. The investigator should talk to the supervisors and possibly to some of the applicant's former co-workers, to get a fuller picture of his employment history.

If personal references are given, the investigator should talk to at least a couple of them. Many people think that an applicant would never put down any personal reference who would give him a bad report. I have found this is not always true. I have talked to some references who say, "You mean that so-and-so gave me for a reference?"

In addition to the references the applicant has given, the investigator should talk to other people who know the applicant. He should visit the neighborhood where the applicant lives. In many cases, the neighborhood check produces the greatest percentage of derogatory information in the investigation. Enough people should be interviewed to provide a fair cross-section of information.

Is the applicant responsible financially? Does he pay his bills, or is he a ˜kip artist? Has he ever been bankrupt? This information is especially important if he is to be involved with company finances.

Any available criminal record information should be checked. Has he ever been convicted of a felony or misdemeanor? These are public records. Arrests are not.

Is the applicant married, divorced, or separated? If the person has been married five or six times, this might indicate an unstable personality undesirable for employment.

If he served in the military, the applicant's service record should be checked.

Obtaining the Information

The best way to conduct a background check is by an "eyeball interview" . . .face-to-face contact. Information may be accepted by telephone when that is the only way it is available. The same applies to letters from educational institutions or past employers. Phone calls and letters are better than no information, but many times people will say things in personal interviews they will not say on the telephone or put in writing.

Letters can be deceiving. I know of one case where a company was having problems with their controller. When her file was checked, it was noticed that all her reference letters looked like they had been typed on the same typewriter. She had typed all of them herself. . .glowing reports. A check with her previous employer showed an entirely different picture.

Investigation Report

A professional security investigator's background report should be totally impartial. The investigator should not judge the case. He should report facts as facts and opinions as opinions. He should evaluate the sources of information carefully before drawing any conclusions. For example, a neighbor lady might report the applicant is "a drunk." Questioned as to why she thinks this, she may reply, "Well, every Saturday he drinks a couple of beers." She may be a member of the W.C.T.U., and obviously this colors her opinion.

Information obtained by the best investigator in the world is worthless unless he can put it into a concise, readable report. The report should be a narrative in clear, plain English, to serve as a tool for management to use in making their decision regarding the applicant.

Evaluation Check List

To facilitate evaluation of the report, a check list may be made up of items to be considered, with different weights given to various items depending on the requirements of the job. The check list might include, for example:

- Did the applicant give any false information?
- Does his employment history indicate instability or "job-hopping"?
- Could the applicant receive a government security clearance if needed?
- Does he have any criminal record?
- Does he have a drinking or drug problem?
- Does he have a record of chronic illness?
- Is there anything in his background which could make him subject to blackmail?

In summary, background investigation, whether done by staff investigators or by an outside agency, will save money in the long run, as well as enable the best use of human resources. It is in the interests of both employer and employee. It is not the whole answer to the problem of internal theft, but it can be a valuable part of a loss prevention program.

John S. Alden

For the past ten years Mr. Alden has been the chief executive officer in General Personnel Investigations, Inc., a nationwide corporation handling industrial and commercial security. Prior to that he had wide and diversified experience in commercial and industrial security, and in local enforcement and federal investigative departments.

Mr. Alden received his B.A. degree from the University of Southern California in psychology and police administration. He is a member of the California Peace Officers Association, the American Society for Industrial Security, and an associate member of the International Association of Chiefs of Police.

Chapter 22

A TEST FOR HONESTY

By George W. Lindberg

The polygraph examination is used in three areas in the modern business community. The first is the use of the polygraph to screen applicants for positions of trust. The second is the use of the polygraph as a method of continuing security by the periodic testing of employees in sensitive work. The third is the use of the polygraph as an investigative aid after the employment crime has been committed.

Applicant Examinations

In our laboratory we conduct approximately 4,000 applicant examinations a year. The polygraph provides a unique investigative facility in this regard. The theory behind the polygraph screening of applicants is the premise that a person who has engaged in thefts from previous employers or has established a pattern of continuing anti-social conduct will, for all practical purposes, continue to exhibit that conduct with a new employer.

Traditionally employers use techniques such as requiring refer-

© 1968, 1975, Security World Publishing Co., Inc.

ences from former employers or from relatives of the applicant, and some conduct retail credit checks and possibly police record searches.

Standard Methods Unreliable

Regrettably, none of these sources of information can be relied upon for accurate information as to honesty.

It's been estimated that approximately only five percent of the persons who commit crimes are recorded as such in the police files. This is particularly true in the area of employment theft, where most commonly the crime is not reported to the police and, in many cases, not even reported to an insurance company. The chances, therefore, are twenty to one against adverse material appearing in police records, even if the police records are available, as they generally are not.

Retail credit information is of little value in assessing integrity, because financial stability is not a *sine qua non* of honesty.

Relatives or the immediate family of the applicant provide prejudiced information, most commonly in favor of the applicant. Occasionally, however, relatives who have an axe to grind will "blackball" a perfectly satisfactory applicant for purposes of personal revenge.

Previous employers have become more and more reluctant to respond candidly to requests for information on work performance by former employees, both because of the threat of lawsuits and because many employers feel that, given a new opportunity, the former employee will reform.

More important, however, is the fact that employees often steal from employers in such a manner that it is never discovered, or discovered only months or years after the employee has been terminated or has left the company.

For example, we recently conducted an examination on an applicant for a position as a security officer in a well-known retail establishment.

During the course of his examination, the initial phases of which he failed to pass, the subject admitted that while working for his previous employer he had stolen approximately $20,000 in merchandise. He assured us that his employer never knew he had stolen this valuable merchandise and, in fact, the former employer had given a fine recommendation of this employee to the new employer.

Written Examination Developed

In our applicant testing program we are aided by a written examination which precedes the polygraph examination. It is called the Reid Report and its concept was developed by John E. Reid while he was the chief examiner at the Chicago Police Scientific Laboratory between 1940 and 1947. After going into private practice, Mr. Reid developed the Reid Report to the point that we are now marketing it without reference to a polygraph examination.

The principal function of the Reid Report is the evaluation of the subject's attitude toward honesty. This is accomplished by the use of approximately 100 questions which the subject must answer with a yes or no. These questions, which have been developed over a 25-year period, are designed to reflect the subject's basic attitude in regard to dishonesty by other persons and by himself. His answers are scored and given individual weights which are then computed to give him an overall score.

Test Comprehensive

The Reid Report provides a detailed analysis of the subject's entire employment history. Additionally a person is requested to provide armed service history, a medical history, and financial history and present status.

The commission of crimes and the person's conviction record, if any, is asked for, and the person is requested to agree to various conditions which will assist in subsequent investigations if losses occur. These include such things as having fingerprints taken, submitting handwriting samples for questioned document examination, and an agreement to undergo polygraph examinations under various conditions.

Test Validated by Polygraph

The Reid Report is a unique pre-employment tool because it has been validated in an unusually effective way. During its early development the Reid Report was completed by the applicant and then he was immediately given a polygraph examination which permitted us to determine the relationship between his Reid Report score and the final results of the polygraph examination. While there was in the earlier years some disparity between the results, the present correlation between the results of the polygraph examination and the results of the Reid Report as revised by several additions is now above 90 percent.

The report is now a standard part of our laboratory pre-employment procedure and is being used to screen for honesty by banks and some of the nation's largest companies.

The Value of the Report

The experience that we have gained by conducting over 20,000 pre-employment polygraph and Reid Report examinations has indicated to us that approximately 30 percent of the population has an attitude that simply will not tolerate dishonesty in the area of theft.

It would be a most desirable situation if it were possible to employ only that 30 percent. The economics of the employment market are such, however, that an additional 40 percent are permitted to obtain positions of trust with but a reasonable degree of risk. The character of the persons in the 40 percent group are such that with reasonable security precautions they will not become involved in dishonest acts such as theft.

The final 30 percent, however, will actually create an opportunity to engage in theft. It is this group that the Reid Report is designed to eliminate from consideration for employment in positions of trust.

Factors in Theft

Our work in this area has indicated that there are three principal factors upon which a person's decision to engage in theft is predicated.

Opportunity: The first is the factor of opportunity. More specifically, the question the employee asks himself is, "What is the opportunity for me to take this item without being caught?" This is obviously the reason why banks have surprise audits and strict accounting procedures. In retail security this is the reason for surveillance and shopping services. It is incumbent upon every business to reduce wherever possible the opportunity for an employee to steal without being caught.

Need: The second factor which is basic to the theft problem is the question of need.

A substantial number of people will refrain from stealing if they are adequately compensated and if they are careful in the expenditure of funds. However, all of us in this field are acutely aware that on occasion unusual expenses arise and this can cause the otherwise reasonably honest employee to cross the line to thievery. This of course is the reason for the importance of financial histories, as well as the basis for concern over the employee's moral character.

Attitude: Finally, there is the all-important character of attitude toward honesty. This was the purpose for which the Reid Report was created. As I pointed out earlier, 30 percent of the population will not steal regardless of need or opportunity, security measures must be maintained for a middle group of approximately 40 percent of the population, whose attitude toward honesty is not so firm, and the Reid Report has established itself as a convenient and effective method for rejecting those persons who fall into the final 30 percent.

Validation Research

With the inception of the Equal Employment Opportunity Commission and other similar bodies, Reid and Associates felt it appropriate to offer proof that the Reid Report did not discriminate as to race, sex or age, as well as to establish the exact validity and reliability factors. To conduct this research, Dr. Philip Ash, a psychologist from the University of Illinois, joined the firm. An active proponent of civil rights and well respected in the employment testing field, Dr. Ash was a member of a committee which helped shape the EEOC guidelines and serves as a consultant to that commission.

His research verified findings that the Reid Report did not adversely affect any protected groups, and established an unusually high validity for a pencil and paper test. This research has been published in professional journals and is available upon written request from John E. Reid and Associates.

George W. Lindberg

Former vice president and legal counsel for John E. Reid and Associates in Chicago, Mr. Lindberg is a graduate of Northwestern University School of Law and is a licensed polygraph examiner. He has conducted more than five thousand polygraph examinations around the world. A member of the Illinois State Bar Association and the American Polygraph Association, he has lectured at many universities.

Mr. Lindberg was elected to two terms in the Illinois General Assembly as State Representative and was appointed to the Illinois Crime Investigating Commission. In 1972 he was elected to a four-year term as State Comptroller of Illinois.

VIII.
INTERNAL
THEFT
CONTROLS

Chapter 23

MANAGEMENT'S ROLE IN EMPLOYEE THEFT PREVENTION

By John Natale

The liaison between management and security is a significant factor contributing to the success of a security division. Within our corporate structure at Vornado, we have reached the mutual understanding that the security division is a vital, functional part of our organization—as important as any retail category.

It is a matter of statistics that the internal theft problem continues to be the most serious element confronting retailers today. In 1973, non-residential burglaries were responsible for the loss of $313 million dollars nationally.[6]

However, employee theft is far more costly than the nation's burglaries, robberies and auto thefts combined. Approximately $3 billion is lost annually by business and industry due to employee pilferage alone.[7]

From a presentation given at the International Security Conference in New York City, 1968.

[6]CRIME IN THE UNITED STATES, 1973, FBI Uniform Crime Reports, p. 20.

[7]Chamber of Commerce of the United States, A HANDBOOK ON WHITE COLLAR CRIME (Washington, D.C., 1974), p. 6.

Full Support of Management Needed

Indications are that the problem will worsen progressively in future years. We are very fortunate at Vornado in that management confronts the shrinkage problem in a serious manner. A coordination of efforts by both management and security has accomplished much in keeping our shrinkage within reason. Unfortunately, however, security departments in most instances are not recognized as an integral part of the management team. Poor management and weak security staffs have contributed to the upswing of internal thefts.

An organization is as effective or as weak as its management. Procedures and policies can only be as strong as those regulating and enforcing them. Without the full support of top management, the security department cannot function as a useful, working part of the retail or industrial organization.

The local store manager, for the most part, controls security. Therefore, security personnel operating where merchandise and cash are being handled cannot be objective in their reviews and their appraisals of existing conditions. Management must be made aware that security can no longer be treated as excess baggage in their budgets, a necessary evil. Losses due to employee thefts will bear this out.

This built-in risk factor of human nature is too often ignored by those members of management who should be most vitally concerned. An organization which makes it necessary for the security department to report to intermediate management rather than top management is gambling with this human risk factor, against heavily weighted odds.

A recent investigation in one of our units involving the general store management subsequently led to the termination of fifteen employees and a tremendous recovery of cash and merchandise. Our security staff in this instance became suspicious of certain developments and requested the assistance of the corporate security office. Had the store level security department been required to report to store level management, obstacles might have been created to prevent this investigation from being brought to a successful conclusion. Details would have been clouded over and important facts would not have been brought to light.

Direct communication in all areas of the organization must be developed and encouraged. Top management must be made aware of the malpractices within the organization, not only by reports from intermediate management, but by reports from the lower echelon as well. For example, store level security should report directly to the home office wherever practical, or to a regional or field supervisor. There must be a clear distinction made in the reporting relationship for security personnel.

Dishonesty Can Occur at Any Level

Some of us become so interested in judging a person by appearance, productivity, and caliber of work, that we often fail to realize the detrimental potential existent within every human being. Therefore, to understand the climate for dishonesty, we as members of management must accept and understand human nature and human fallibility, even within the managerial structure.

In a recent study, we learned that 65% of employee thefts uncovered were traced to supervisory and executive personnel. A recent case in point involved a manager of bogus check collection. A sizable shortage in the collection moneys automatically placed suspicion on the manager. Here again, the importance of chain of communication was brought to our attention. We could only speculate on the outcome of this investigation had security been required to report directly to intermediate management. A restricted chain of communication could easily have made it possible for this individual to conceal his dishonest activities and continue to defraud the company without fear of detection or interruption.

The internal theft problem cannot be solved by waving a magic wand. There are not enough gimmicks or gadgets available to eliminate the problem. But it can be systematically reduced and controlled. Management's first error is allowing symptoms to appear before taking aggressive and corrective action. "What's in it for me?" is too often the watchword of today's working man. One may justify wrong-doing by rationalizing it away as something one is entitled to. When this "What's in it for me?" attitude reaches and infiltrates management, a serious structural weakness exists. How, then, can the average working man be expected to follow the standards set forth by management, when those standards are considerably lowered by the varying degrees of human susceptibility?

We must recognize that as the opportunity for dishonesty increases within the organization, the number of persons who reach the point where opportunity cannot be resisted will also become greater. And we find this apparent in every phase of the organizational structure. A recent investigation which resulted in the termination of five employees included an area supervisor, a department manager, and three salesmen, all in the same department. An observation by security led to the termination of two employees, which disclosed the involvement of the others through implications made. This investigation alone realized a cash recovery to the company of over $4,000.

No one is immune to temptation, from the sales girl who pockets the difference of an under-ring, to the general store manager who manipulates large sums of money or merchandise for his own personal gain. Weak management begets poor relationships within an organization. Poor relationships open the way to lack of respect, which can, if allowed to exist, break away the cornerstone and in time crumble the organizational structure.

Help to Reduce Temptation

A double standard of business ethics cannot be tolerated. A clerk must know and be certain that a department manager would receive the same disciplinary action as he himself would if found to have committed a dishonest or fraudulent act. The majority of employees first come to work with good records, but because of laxity on the part of management, and a weak security staff, they inevitably become thieves. The temptations are great; an effective, efficient security department can help reduce that temptation.

Management must have a continuous feedback regarding theft in each of their units, regardless of location or size. And top management must take an active interest in all phases of the operation. It is necessary that company policies and operating procedures are met with complete compliance in all areas—managerial, supervisorial and lower echelon. Companies spend small fortunes to combat shoplifting. If the same efforts were exerted toward handling their internal problems, much would be done to reduce retail losses.

Need for Trained Personnel

Management must be made to understand that we are dealing in a very sensitive and complex area which requires experienced and trained security specialists to cope with problems confronting us today. We must be competitive with law enforcement agencies to attract the caliber and quality of personnel needed in this area.

Training of new security personnel is a painstaking and time-consuming task. However, with security specialists in supervisory capacity readily available, we are assured of success with a minimum of time lost. The use of highly trained personnel results in a savings to an organization by gaining maximum results with a minimum of expenditure through payroll and miscellaneous expenses. The presence of a well-trained, well-organized security staff within the organization is a recognized benefit. However, in order for management to accept security as a vital necessity, substantial, irrefutable evidence must be presented.

It is evident, then, that a security division must maintain and organize an up-to-date system of recording every phase of the department's responsibilities. A dependable and systematic filing and reporting system is a must. From these individual reports, the main office can formulate a monthly, quarterly, and yearly analysis to present to top management which would justify the very presence of the security division. In so doing, management has before them indisputable statistics as to security's work. We can show in figures representing actual recoveries to the company exactly what security has accomplished on a profit-and-loss basis—and this has nothing to do with the improvement of the shrinkage percentage, where there are many factors that contribute to a shrinkage.

In presenting a program to management, where recoveries are involved, results should be emphasized on a profit and loss basis. For example, in 1974 we were responsible for recovering 51% of the total payroll we spent on security.

A self-contained, thorough security division is an even greater savings to an organization by utilizing available personnel for surveillance, undercover work, and shopping services. Several years ago we added a trained polygraphist to our staff, and we have enjoyed results not possible before. When we asked for two additional polygraphists, management granted this request without hesitation because of the successful results which we were able to obtain. Recoveries to date from these important additions have more than compensated for the initial investment, and we foresee unlimited possibilities.

A security division that has the full support and cooperation of top management in combatting the internal theft problems can be assured of gratifying results.

John Natale

Mr. Natale has been in the retail security field for over 20 years. He joined Montgomery-Ward in 1951 and was the Eastern Regional Security Manager for that organization. He became Security Director for Vornado, Inc., in 1962. He joined City Stores Corporation as a Security Director in 1964 and returned to Vornado as Assistant Vice-President in charge of security in 1967.

He holds a B.A. degree in pre-law from Marshall University and has attended Fairleigh Dickinson University and New York University.

Mr. Natale has been a speaker and a participant in many national and regional seminars. He is a member of the International Association of Chiefs of Police, the New Jersey State Association of Chiefs of Police, Police Chiefs of Southeastern Pennsylvania, and the Society of Investigators of Greater Newark.

Chapter 24

EMBEZZLEMENT CONTROLS

By Lester A. Pratt

I.

No employer likes to consider the possibility that dishonesty on the part of one or more of his employees may someday cause him a serious loss. Small employers, especially, are inclined to minimize their exposure to losses of this character. Nevertheless, it is a known fact that many thousands of persons in positions of trust and responsibility do "go wrong" every year, often with disastrous results to their employers.

Statistics as to the total annual embezzlement losses in this country are necessarily incomplete because the implications of this crime are such as to cause many of its victims to refrain from publicizing their ill fortune. However, a careful review of all

Reprinted by permission of Fidelity and Deposit Company of Maryland, distributors of the pamphlet from which this article was taken, "Embezzlement Controls for Business Enterprises." The material was reprinted, with permission, in SECURITY WORLD Magazine in 1966. Copies of the pamphlet can be obtained from: Fidelity and Deposit Company of Maryland, Advertising and Public Relations Dept., 208 Fidelity Building, Baltimore, Maryland 21203.

available information on the subject convincingly indicates that stealing by employees is costing American business enterprises upwards of one billion dollars a year. This is a staggering tribute to pay to dishonesty and clearly suggests an alarming degree of inefficiency in the average firm's defenses against employee frauds.

This fact stands out: no one has yet discovered a sure-fire method of avoiding the employment of potential embezzlers. Embezzlers follow no pattern, show no recognizable outward signs. They may be 18 or 80, work for an employer four months or forty years, be paid $1,800 or $18,000 and steal anywhere from a few hundred dollars to many hundreds of thousands. For the most part, embezzlements are committed by individuals who have no previous criminal records and whose business and personal backgrounds are beyond reproach.

Nevertheless, an employer should investigate all prospective employees. This should include inquiries to former employers. Also, an employer should keep abreast of his employees' mode of living, habits, domestic lives and friends. It is surprising how effective this is in the prevention and detection of losses.

There are two elements in the crime of embezzlement. One is management's sin; the other is the embezzler's contribution. The first is temptation. If, in the course of his work, an employee is constantly faced with the opportunity to steal, either through inadequate accounting procedures and/or lack of proper internal control, that's one element. Add to this the second element—a sudden overwhelming need or desire for more money—and the stage is set for embezzlement.

Moral Obligation

In addition to providing decent working conditions, reasonable hours, adequate wages and opportunities for advancement, employers have a definite moral obligation to safeguard their employees' integrity by doing everything possible to deter them from yielding to the temptation to take dishonest advantage of their positions. While no system of accounting or internal control has yet been devised that will absolutely prevent embezzlement, nevertheless much can be done to keep an inherently honest individual from misusing his employer's money in a moment of weakness, or under the stress of financial worry.

Determine Weak Links

Management's first approach to the problem of controlling dishonesty losses should be to determine the weak links in its defenses against this type of employee fraud. The simplest and easiest way to obtain this needed information is to follow a definite survey program. If such a program is carried out and the results of the survey are acted upon intelligently, management can rest assured that its exposure to inside thefts has been minimized.

Who should handle the actual work of making the survey? Obviously, he should be someone well-acquainted with the various operations of the business. In a small business, the owner or manager would be the most logical person. On the other hand, if the business employs well-qualified outside auditors to make semi-annual or annual examinations, the work of making the survey should be assigned to them. This task, however, should be treated as a separate assignment, rather than as part of a regular examination, because it is difficult to combine the work of the two investigations due to their different natures.

In any case, such a survey should embrace a thorough investigation of employment practices, as well as methods of handling receipts and disbursements, collection of accounts receivable, customers' accounts, credits and rebates, bank deposits, petty cash funds, payroll checks, inventories, and all other operations wherein dishonesty losses might originate or occur.

The various controls and other safeguards suggested on the following pages are not intended to represent an ideal dishonesty loss prevention program. They do represent the fundamentals of such a program and as such are indicative of the points to which particular attention should be paid in making a survey of the character proposed above.

How Employees Steal

The ways in which employees may misappropriate money or other property of their employers are limited only by their ingenuity. Such thefts may range from the simple pocketing of an expensive tool to the most intricate accounting manipulation. Following are some of the more common methods of embezzling money:

1. Issuance of checks in payment of bills of fictitious suppliers and cashing them through a dummy, or by faked endorsements.

2. Invoicing goods below established prices and getting cash "kickbacks" from the purchasers.

3. Raising the amounts of checks, invoices and vouchers after they have been officially approved.

4. Issuing and cashing checks for returned purchases not actually returned.

5. Pocketing the proceeds of cash sales and not recording the transactions.

6. Pocketing collections made on presumably uncollectible accounts.

7. "Lapping," i.e., pocketing small amounts from incoming payments and applying subsequent remittances on other items to cover the shortages.

8. Forging checks and destroying them when returned by the bank, then concealing the transactions by forcing footings in the cash books or by raising the amounts of legitimate checks.

9. Charging customers more than the duplicate sales slips show and pocketing the difference.

10. Padding payrolls as to rates, time, production or number of employees.

11. Failing to record returned purchases, allowances and discounts and appropriating equivalent amounts of cash.

12. Paying creditors' invoices twice and appropriating the second check.

13. Appropriating checks made payable to "cash" or bank— supposedly for creditors' accounts, payment of notes or other expenses.

14. Stealing from the cash register and tampering with the tape.

15. Misappropriating cash and charging the amounts taken to fictitious customers' accounts.

16. Increasing the amounts of creditors' invoices and pocketing the excess or splitting with an accomplice employed by the creditors.

17. Pocketing unclaimed wages or dividends.

18. Pocketing portions of collections made from customers and offsetting them on the books by improper credits for allowances or discounts.

Cash Receipt Control

Cash receipts require the fullest possible measure of control. Misappropriations of such receipts may be accomplished either before or after they have been recorded. Generally speaking, it is easier to detect an embezzlement of cash if some record of its receipt exists. Consequently, in carrying out a fraud exposure survey, special attention should be paid to the precautions employed to prevent thefts of unrecorded cash receipts, such as cash sales and collections on customers' accounts.

Cash registers, pre-numbered sales tickets in pad or book form and autographic registers are the three most common safeguards employed in handling of over-the-counter receipts.

If cash registers are used, each sales clerk preferably should be assigned his own machine and twice a day each register should be cleared by a responsible official of all cash above a set amount required for making change. Sales clerks should never be permitted to have access to the keys to the locking mechanisms of their registers.

If pre-numbered sales tickets are used, they should be made out in duplicate or triplicate and each sales person should be held accountable for each ticket in his pad or book. At the close of each day, the total of the amounts indicated on the sales tickets should balance with the total amount of cash received by the cashier. To avoid falsification of the sales tickets, at the time of making each sale, both the original and duplicate tickets should be sent to the cashier to be stamped "Paid."

There are a number of autographic registers, or sales-receipting machines, on the market. In general, such devices involve the use of pre-numbered sales tickets which are turned out by a crank, each revolution depositing a copy of the filled-out ticket in a locked compartment. These copies should be removed and checked daily by a responsible official with the amount of cash received by the cashier.

Cash Receipts

The receiving, opening and distribution of incoming mail should be handled by, or under the supervision of, a responsible official other than the cashier or bookkeeper. This person should make a list of all receipts, both cash and checks, showing from whom received, amounts, etc. This list preferably should be made in duplicate on numbered forms, both copies being signed by the person opening the mail and by the cashier to whom the receipts are delivered. The original is retained by the cashier and the duplicate is sent to the auditing or accounting department for filing.

To prevent falsification of cash book entries, each day's list of incoming receipts should be carefully checked against such entries to make sure that they agree.

Because embezzlements of cash often are concealed by underfooting the cash receipts book totals, these footings should be verified at least weekly.

All incoming remittances and other cash receipts should be deposited in the bank intact and each day's receipts should agree with the daily deposits.

All checks received should be stamped "for deposit only" and deposited within 24 hours after they are received.

Bank deposits should be accompanied by three deposit slips, one of which should be stamped by the bank and immediately returned to the person making the deposit for subsequent delivery to the cashier. The other should be mailed by the bank direct to the depositor's auditing department. The third copy is retained by the bank for its record of the deposit.

Each day's deposit slips should be checked against the day's list of remittances and cash receipts.

Bank statements should be received and reconciled by someone other than the person who is responsible for preparing deposits, or empowered to make deposits or withdrawals, or who is in charge of accounting for receipts and disbursements. All canceled checks should be carefully examined for possible evidence of alteration, as well as to make sure they have been properly endorsed by the payees. If any errors, erasures or alterations appear on the statement, the bank should be asked to furnish a duplicate.

Unless absolutely unavoidable, the duties of cashier and bookkeeper should be divided between two people, neither of whom should be permitted access to the other's records.

Proceeds from the sale of waste paper, scrap and similar items may amount to a considerable sum in the course of a year and should be carefully watched since such sales are usually made on a bargaining basis and for cash.

Other Good Accounting Practices

All non-cash entries covering allowances, bad debts, discounts, returns, etc., should be made, or at least approved, by a responsible official other than the cashier or bookkeeper.

Before charging off an account as uncollectible, a check should be made to determine whether or not the customer in question actually exists. All accounts regarded as collectible should be transferred to a memorandum control account and periodically reviewed, because subsequent collections on such accounts often add up to sizable amounts.

Accounts receivable should be sampled, or test-checked, from time to time by having some person other than the ledger clerk prepare and mail statements to all such accounts.

Employees who handle credit memos and other adjustments with customers should not be permitted access to the accounts receivable records.

Where the size of the organization permits, another desirable safeguard is to require the ledger clerks in the credit and collection department to switch positions every now and then.

Customers' unpaid balances should be verified at least once a year. Positive type verifications should be personally mailed and received by the auditor, or by a responsible official. If any customers fail to acknowledge or return these verifications an investigation should be made to determine if such customers actually exist.

Bookkeepers should not be permitted to make arbitrary adjustments to bring customers' ledgers into balance with the general ledger account.

Entries in the cash book should be made by someone other than the person who reconciles the bank account, or who checks the cash on hand.

Payments on notes receivable should be received by one person and entered by another.

Periodic Examinations

The importance of having periodic examinations made by competent outside certified public accountants cannot be overemphasized. These audits should be made at least annually and should include an examination of inventory schedules as to prices, extensions, footings and such further tests as the situation may require. The audit program also should cover a comprehensive examination and verification of all assets, liability, net worth, income and expense accounts. Occasional surprise audits also are highly desirable.

II.

Effective internal control of the disbursements of funds is somewhat simpler than for cash receipts.

All disbursements, except for a "petty cash fund," should be made by check.

All checks issued should be serially numbered and written either on a check-writing machine or in permanent ink on safety paper.

Countersignature is highly desirable, and authority to sign or countersign should be delegated to not more than two responsible officials.

If an error is made in writing a check, the check should be voided and another issued.

Cash disbursement records should be independently footed and checked to the related general ledger control accounts.

Petty Cash Fund

Control of this money should begin with the establishment of a specific fund sufficient to meet the daily requirements of business and this amount should be entered in the general ledger.

No disbursements should be made from this fund without a supporting voucher, approved by a responsible official and signed by the person receiving the cash. To prevent alteration, these vouchers preferably should be typewritten, or made out in permanent ink and the amounts written out in full, i.e., ten dollars, not $10.00.

Wherever possible, original invoices of vendors should be attached to the petty cash vouchers supporting such disbursements.

The fund should be replenished from time to time by drawing a check in the amount of the paid vouchers in the drawer. At this time, someone other than the employee in charge of the fund should inspect the vouchers for possible evidence of fraud and they should be cancelled by perforation, date stamp, or in some other satisfactory manner so as to prevent their possible re-use.

Frequent unannounced inspections of the vouchers in the petty cash drawer should be made by a responsible official and the fund balanced. This procedure will have the effect of minimizing the risk of petty embezzlements and do much to prevent employees from obtaining unauthorized cash advances.

As a guard against the possibility of an employee increasing the amount of an invoice after its payment, then entering the increased figure on the books and pocketing the difference from miscellaneous cash, all paid purchase invoices should be checked from time to time to make sure that totals have not been altered.

Cash receipts should never be commingled with the petty cash fund.

Purchasing

Wherever the size of the organization permits, the purchasing of all merchandise, either for re-sale or for use in a store or plant, should be centralized. Pre-numbered requisitions should be used to originate the purchasing activity. These should be prepared in triplicate, the original going to the vendor, the duplicate retained in the unfilled order file and the triplicate sent to the receiving clerk. In preparing the latter copy, a short carbon should be used so that the quantity ordered is left blank, making it subsequently necessary for the receiving clerk to insert the quantity actually received.

When the triplicate copy is received by the person in charge of purchasing, the quantity of merchandise or materials indicated is checked with the vendor's invoice and attached to it. The duplicate copy is then taken from the unfilled order file, checked as to price and extensions with the vendor's invoice and filed in the filled-orders file for future reference. The vendor's invoice is ready for official approval for entry in the firm's accounting records and subsequent payment.

Checks issued in payment of purchases should be accompanied by the applicable purchase invoice and the latter should be initialed by both the person signing the checks and by the countersigner.

Wherever possible, purchasing and receiving functions should be kept entirely separate, so as to minimize the risk of collusion between a vendor and the purchasing agent, to guard against short shipments of merchandise, and, in general, to hold the receiving clerk accountable for all merchandise delivered by the vendor.

Further protection is obtained when a third person, *viz.*, the owner or someone in a supervisory position, takes an active interest in checking purchase invoices for prices, description of goods purchased, quality, quantity, extension of costs, footings, discounts, transportation charges, etc. At least a selective test should be made of all invoices relating to purchases of materials in large quantities and money value.

Competitive Bids

Wherever practicable, competitive bids should be required for the purchase of large quantities of goods to guard against a vendor being given orders at an excessive price, or for inferior quality, with a subsequent cash "kickback" to the person in charge of purchasing.

When vendors' invoices are paid, they should be stamped "Paid" and both the check numbers and dates of payment noted on the invoices.

Where accommodation purchases are made for the benefit of employees, management should make sure that payment for such items is collected from the employees, either by payroll deductions or cash, and not charged to some expense account.

In the case of purchases made on behalf of customers, with delivery to be made direct by the vendors to the customers, certain safeguards also are necessary to make sure that such orders are properly accounted for and billed to the customers. It usually will suffice in such cases to make a notation on the vendor's invoice to show that the customer has been billed, as well as the date and number of the bill. There have been many cases where a bookkeeper or other clerical employee has deliberately failed to bill a customer in return for a cash "kickback" from the latter.

Returned purchases may be adequately safeguarded by putting into reverse the system previously suggested with respect to the purchase of merchandise or materials for use in the plant or store.

Many large losses have been caused through duplicate payment of creditors' invoices. In most such cases, the defaulter will select invoices which were paid in previous years and only change the year date. After the check in payment of the falsified invoice has been signed, the defaulter will either forge the endorsement, or perhaps be in collusion with the payee to collect the proceeds of the check. Consequently, creditors' invoices should always be carefully checked before payment to make sure that they have not been falsified in any way.

Payrolls

Where it is practicable to do so, employees should be paid by checks, preferably of a different color than those used for other purposes. It also is desirable that a statement of each employee's earnings and applicable deductions appear on a perforated extension of the check form.

Where employees are paid by cash and a large number of individuals are involved, it is preferable for the employer to arrange with his bank to prepare the payroll.

Current cash receipts should never be used for payroll purposes.

Wherever possible, the preparation of the payroll and paying off of employees should be handled by different employees, especially if the employees are paid in cash.

If a separate bank account is used for payroll purposes only, the bank statement and canceled payroll checks should be sent for reconciliation direct to a principal administrative employee who does not participate in the actual preparation of the payroll.

After an appropriate interval—a week is usual—all unclaimed pay should be turned back to the treasurer or other similar official for re-deposit in the bank. It is highly important that unclaimed pay be investigated to disclose any irregularities that may exist as the result of "payroll padding."

Time cards which show erasures of dates should be carefully checked as a guard against the re-use of previously honored cards.

Verification

In concerns large enough to be departmentalized, the payroll should be supported by time sheets signed by the department heads. These should be made subject to verification by persons not members of the departments concerned.

The timekeeper who checks employees in at a plant in the morning should not also check them out at night.

Rates of pay, time worked and computations of amounts earned should be reviewed independently at selected intervals. Surprise examinations are the most effective.

Administrative officials should examine any abnormal increase in the number of employees, rates and labor costs.

Officials should not sign payroll checks in blank for emergency use during their absence.

All payroll checks voided for any reason should be retained for examination and audit. They should be mutilated and the signatures torn off so that they cannot be used.

Payroll time cards also should be canceled in such a way as to prevent their possible re-use.

When a new employee is hired, the employment office or personnel department, as the case may be, should immediately furnish the payroll division with the employee's name, address, title, salary, etc., and this notification should be signed by a responsible officer. To prevent "payroll padding," the same procedure also should be followed when an employee leaves the company.

From time to time, the payroll should be checked to make sure that the number of names corresponds to the number of employees.

Another good check is for the internal auditor at periodic intervals, or the certified public accountant at the time of audit, to deliver personally pay checks or pay envelopes to all employees or on a spot-check basis by using a pre-determined percentage of them. This has the effect of having the employee identify himself and is another means of preventing "payroll padding."

Distribution of the W-2 forms annually to employees by the internal auditor or the certified public accountant will accomplish the same purpose.

Merchandise Controls

In most cases, embezzlements of merchandise are made possible by the lack of proper controls over the following operations: (1) receiving, (2) delivery, and (3) inventory.

Wherever possible, the duties of receiving, storekeeping and delivery should be handled by three different individuals.

Generally speaking, controlling the receipt of merchandise or materials is accomplished in the same manner previously described under "Purchasing." Having acknowledged receipt of the goods on the triplicate copy of the purchase order, the receiving clerk then is charged with the custodianship of the property, unless he discharges his responsibility in this respect by delivery of the goods to a storekeeper.

The same procedure should be followed with respect to transfers of merchandise from stockrooms to sales departments. Here again pre-numbered vouchers or requisitions should be used, receipted by the sales clerks and the transfers entered on the inventory records. If the stock numbers are indicated on the sales slips, a perpetual inventory of merchandise in each sales unit can be maintained.

Similar controls over work in process or material sent to jobs away from the plant may be adopted by means of pre-numbered job requisitions.

Where all three duties—receiving, storekeeping and delivery— are performed by a single employee, a perpetual inventory should be maintained by some other clerical employee. In no case should the person in charge of the stockroom also be in charge or have access to the perpetual inventory records.

Acknowledging receipt of merchandise is by no means a "cure-all" in preventing theft of incoming goods. Frequent physical inspections or test-checks of the storeroom to verify the quantity of merchandise on hand should be made by someone other than the person in charge of receiving, storing and delivery of the materials.

Delivery

Controlling the delivery of merchandise to customers is a problem that affects both large and small firms. Both internal and external controls are necessary to curtail losses arising out of this operation. In most cases, such losses are collusive frauds, one or more confederates participating with the defaulter.

Inside employees usually have the best opportunities for initiating this type of theft. For example, an inside employee of a wholesale meat company, who had access to the refrigerator, would arrange to place quantities of meat on a driver's truck in excess of the amount required for deliveries to regular customers. The driver would sell this extra meat for cash to various markets and split the proceeds with his accomplice. Discovery of the thefts came about only as the result of a tip by a discharged employee.

Rotation of the employees who loaded the meat trucks, or careful spot checking at irregular intervals, would have quickly brought this condition to light and stopped further losses.

Where merchandise is sold and is to be delivered, satisfactory control usually can be accomplished by the use of pre-numbered shipping tickets on which should be listed all the items included in the order, signed or initialed by the shipping clerk and also by the transporter, *viz.*, the employer's driver or the operator of a common carrier, at the time the merchandise is placed in the vehicle. A copy of the receipted ticket should be sent to the accounting department for entry on its sales and inventory records.

Inventory

Inventories are customarily taken at monthly, semi-annual, or annual intervals, depending upon the size and type of business concerned. Where perpetual inventory records are maintained by someone outside the storekeeping department, it is possible to exercise effective control over withdrawals of merchandise from the stockroom through the use of pre-numbered requisitions prepared in duplicate. A selective physical count of certain items in stock can then be made on a weekly or monthly basis and compared with the balance shown on the inventory record cards. Any difference should be carefully checked to determine the cause.

In the taking of a physical inventory, sales clerks should inventory merchandise in departments other than the ones where they are regularly employed and persons from departments other than the stockroom should be used in taking the physical inventory of that division. Physical inventories should be made entirely independent of the perpetual inventory records and the results of each such inventory should be checked with the perpetual inventory by a responsible officer.

Failure to properly control the activities of porters, messengers, charwomen, janitors and other similar employees may lead to large inventory losses. For example, a porter employed by a wholesale liquor dealer made a practice of filling old cartons and trash containers with pint bottles of whisky. An accomplice, driving what purported to be an ice truck, picked up the loot after hours and delivered it to a certain grocery store. The confederates split the proceeds, which amounted to $35 for each case delivered.

In another case, a porter for a wholesale tobacco dealer after hours would drop cases of cigarettes and cigars out of the storeroom windows to confederates in the alley below, who would dispose of them to various small merchants in the neighborhood. This loss amounted to approximately $65,000 over a period of three years.

The proper control of inventories, with frequent surprise spot checks of merchandise, coupled with storerooms provided with protected windows and doors, will ordinarily prevent losses of this character.

III.

Many retail businesses may employ only one office clerk who combines all the various functions of bookkeeping with the collection and disbursement of funds and the custody of various assets. This also is true of many small manufacturing plants whose entire office force may consist of not more than two or three persons.

Since internal control requires the employment of enough people to permit the work to be divided in such a manner as to afford little opportunity for inside thievery without collusion, it is obvious that some other plan must be utilized in small businesses to control employee dishonesty. The most practical method calls for the owner to assume some of the duties of an internal auditor, such as scrutiny of transactions, confirmation of items and investigation of original documents and the amounts and entries which result from them.

Controls for Small Business

In all such cases, it is possible for the owner to institute a program of internal audit to compensate for the lack of internal control. Such a program would embrace the following procedures:

1. All cash receipts should be deposited intact daily.
2. All disbursements should be made by check, countersigned by the owner or manager, except such small disbursements as are made from a petty cash fund.
3. Bank accounts should be reconciled by the owner monthly.

4.   Occasionally, outgoing customers' statements should be verified with the accounts receivable ledger and mailed by the owner.

5.   The owner should receive and open the mail, particularly during the first few days of each month.

6.   The owner should compare all cash receipts with his books and the deposits shown on the bank statement.

7.   Receiving and shipping of merchandise should be done by someone other than the bookkeeper and carefully checked by the owner.

8.   All journal entries should receive the approval of the owner, especially those having to do with returned sales, allowances and bad debts.

Frequently, the owner of a small business will claim that he does carry out such a program. While he may be honest in his opinion, it has been observed in many instances that his failure to understand the principles of responsibility and accountability has resulted in his not checking some significant step, thus leaving the way wide open for employee dishonesty.

On other occasions, the owner of such a business will claim that he makes regular tests or surprise audits of various accounting phases. It is true, of course, that a systematic program of surprise tests may represent an effective form of internal control or audit, particularly in a small organization. But for such a program to be effective it must first of all be a *program*. Secondly, it must be operated on a predetermined plan in order that the element of surprise actually may be present. If the owner actually does maintain a written program against which he has recorded the dates of his various tests, then his claim may appear credible. Unfortunately, many businessmen think that they are vigilant when, as a matter of fact, they have been lulled into complacency and trustfulness.

The owner of every business with an office force of only one or two "trusted employees" should remember that these conditions present a most fertile field for employee dishonesty, and until he has satisfied himself that the internal audit has actually been of such a character as to remedy the deficiencies in internal control, he should carry out the program previously outlined.

Electronic Data Processing

The most obvious advantage in using electronic data processing equipment is its capacity to digest, process and record masses of data at great speed and reliability. This capacity may also be a source of great vulnerability from a loss standpoint due to honest and dishonest mistakes. Its reliability may be likened to fire and water—good servants but bad masters.

Perhaps the greatest area of vulnerability in utilizing a computer system, except from that caused by an honest mistake or a dishonest act, is the accidental destruction of media contained on the reels of magnetic tapes, memory drums, punched paper tapes, cards, etc., and the inability to reconstruct or the necessity to reconstruct at great expense.

The importance of safeguarding the "concentration of values," represented in the information stored in such media from destruction by fire, or other casualty, is brought out by the facts on the fire at the Pentagon in which three computers in the Air Force Statistical Division Offices were destroyed. The loss by fire was nearly seven million dollars. To re-create the information on the 7,000 reels would increase the loss to thirty million dollars.

Under automation, the three general operating areas are clerical, programming and the running of the computer. Duties should be segregated to assure good control. For example, one individual should not, in the ordinary course of events, have full responsibility over a transaction. Programming might be defined as telling the computer how to do the job, while the computer operator's job can be described as punching the buttons. Actually, the operators should not be programmers.

In an automated installation, a poorly conceived computer operation can be as costly and dangerous as fraud. Management must be very alert to this possibility.

Internal Controls

Controlling the purpose and use of the E.D.P. equipment is important. Management should also control computer activity to avoid unauthorized use of the equipment. For example, the manager of the computer department of a large company utilized the equipment on Saturdays and Sundays to process work for other organizations, without the authority of his employer, and retained the fees for such services. Actually, he operated as a one-man service center at the expense of his employer.

Internal control consists of the checks and balances established by management to safeguard the assets, provide reliable financial statements and obtain adherence to management policies.

Controlling the Flow of Data

This departs from the usual horizontal level of internal accounting controls whereby, for example, the work of the accounts receivable clerk checks the work of the sales analysis clerk, which in turn operates as a check on the materials charged out by the perpetual inventory clerk.

Control of the flow of data can be achieved by separating the following duties:

1. The initiation of accounting data.
2. The processing and accumulating of the data.
3. The ultimate summary recording and review of the data.

In relation to the operation of the machine system, this division of duties can be expressed as control of the initiation and input of the data to the system, control of the machine operation and control applied to the output of the system.

Input Controls

Input controls are concerned with insuring that the input data properly reflect all transactions occurring and that the transactions are authorized by appropriate officials. For example, all material received should be properly recorded on a receiving report which has been authorized by a purchase order. Some input control techniques are:

1. Accumulating control totals prior to the introduction of the data into the system.

2. Insuring that data are accurately transcribed into a form that can be read by the system.

The importance of good input controls is demonstrated by the ease with which an employee in a brokerage firm using electronic data processing equipment transferred to his personal trading account interest income by the substitution of punched cards before the tapes were updated.

Output Controls

The function of output controls is to determine that the processed data do not include any unauthorized alterations by the machine operation group and that they are substantially correct or reasonable. It is desirable that the personnel responsible for the output controls have no control of the physical assets involved, the detail records, the machine operation of the authorization of transactions. Some output control techniques are:

1. Comparison of control totals of data processed with summary totals obtained independently from original source data; total of dollar amounts, count of items for processing, cash totals of quantities or identification numbers. This should be considered the basic control.
2. Control by exception:
   a. Investigation of exceptions or limit violations produced by the machine operation.
   b. Investigation of differences revealed by periodic physical inventories and communications from customers.
   c. Comparison of totals with totals of the prior period and summaries of intervening changes.
   d. Statistical analysis of totals (gross profit percentages, average hourly rate, etc.)
3. Systematic sampling of the accuracy and propriety of individual items processed, originating tests both from input and output records.
4. Submission of reports and analyses of processed data to originating group for their review and check of unusual or abnormal items.

A new set of problems of internal control are presented by processing on electronic data processing systems. The seriousness of these problems will vary directly with the extent by which management, through imaginative planning, controls the system. Management also has a responsibility to assure that all personnel associated with a data processing system are fully informed as to the capabilities and limitations of the system.

Honesty Bond Insurance

Even under the most ideal system of internal control and auditing, losses through employee dishonesty may still occur. This is only natural, because no such systems can be any stronger than the individuals who operate them. When the human element breaks down, the system is bound to fail, too. Accordingly, prudent employers will take the added precaution of purchasing and maintaining adequate honesty bond insurance.

The cost of this protection is small, the benefits considerable. Honesty bond insurance not only indemnifies employers for losses caused by the dishonest acts of employees, but also serves as a strong deterrent to wrongdoing. Furthermore, the knowledge that they may be subject to investigation by an insurance company often keeps dishonest persons from seeking employment with businesses known to carry honesty bond insurance.

The question of how much of this type of insurance to carry always arises when this coverage is discussed and it is not an easy one to answer. It is largely a matter of individual judgment and the heads of a business are the ones who should assume the responsibility of making the final decision. One thing is certain: in considering the question of how much protection to carry, employers should think in terms of possible losses big enough to do them serious harm, not in terms of such inconsiderable losses as might result from petty pilfering.

The Surety Association of America, a trade association whose members are the nation's principal underwriters of honesty bond insurance, has developed a practical method for determining an employer's minimum honesty insurance requirements. This method is based on the calculation of an employer's "Dishonesty Exposure Index," a factor derived from current assets and gross sales or income, the two principal elements of employee dishonesty exposure. The former element is a measure of the values subject to loss at all times; the latter reflects turnover.

Figure 1 shows how the Employer's Dishonesty Exposure Index may be calculated.

Although many large embezzlement losses involve forgery, and forgery insurance is a valuable and recommended supplement to honesty insurance, such forgery protection should not be relied upon as taking the place of needed honesty bond insurance.

The Dishonesty Exposure Index, applied to the table (Figure 2), will indicate the suggested minimum amount of honesty bond insurance the employer requires. This minimum should be adjusted upward as the employer's special circumstances or exposures require.

Preparation of Claims

Preparing a claim for the total loss sustained and coming within the provisions of a bond is usually not an easy task, even when the person doing the work is familiar with methods commonly employed by embezzlers to conceal their crimes. The majority of defaulters use well-defined plans in misappropriating funds, but innumerable methods are used in the attempts to conceal misappropriations. It is the method used to conceal the act rather than the proof of loss. The methods used by a clever thief are often most easily followed; however, it is very difficult to follow the reasoning of one not so clever.

Many lawsuits and the resulting expenses could be avoided if claims were properly prepared, covering only those losses which are covered by the bond. It should be kept in mind that the burden of proof rests entirely on the Insured and not on the bonding company. Too often reliance is placed on the confession of the embezzler. A confession is normally accepted as evidence of dishonesty but not as to the extent of the loss. The best type of evidence will usually be found by a searching examination of the records of the company. This requires time, patience and experience, but in the end it is the shortest and least expensive procedure to follow. A bonding company will recognize and promptly pay a valid claim if the loss is incurred under the terms of its bond and sufficient proof is submitted to substantiate the loss.

If the claim is litigated in the courts, the expense will be great and the loss in the end must still be substantiated. There are, of course, many cases on record that have been taken to court as a result of a doubtful point of law. In this connection, it is important that the proof of loss and the supporting report be prepared with the thought in mind that both must stand the test in court.

Figure 1

DISHONESTY EXPOSURE INDEX

I.   Enter the employer's total Current Assets (cash, deposits, securities, receivables, goods on hand, etc.) . . . . $ _____

   A.   Value of goods on hand (raw materials, materials in process, finished merchandise or products). . $ _____

   B.   Enter 5% of IA. . . . . $ _____

   C.   Enter Current Assets less Goods On Hand, i.e., the difference between I and IA. . . . . $ _____

   D.   Enter 20% of IC . . . . $ _____

II. Enter Annual Gross Sales or Income. . . . . $ _____

III. Enter 10% of II . . . . $ _____

THIS TOTAL IS THE EMPLOYER'S DISHONESTY EXPOSURE INDEX . . . . $ _____

Note: For businesses which perform service functions, such as transporting the property of others, or which perform work on or process the property of others, or which have such property in their custody, the value of such property should be included in the Current Assets and Goods on Hand totals.

In the case of those acting in representative capacity or otherwise having in their custody or control cash, securities, commercial paper or similar valuables, such values should be included in the Current Assets total.

Figure 2

SUGGESTED MINIMUM AMOUNTS
OF HONESTY INSURANCE

EXPOSURE INDEX		AMOUNT OF COVERAGE	
Up to . . .	$ 25,000	$ 15,000 . . .	.25,000
25,000	125,000	25,000 . . .	.50,000
125,000	250,000	50,000 . . .	.75,000
250,000	500,000	75,000 . . .	100,000
500,000	750,000	100,000 . . .	125,000
750,000 . . .	1,000,000	125,000 . . .	150,000
1,000,000 . . .	1,375,000	150,000 . . .	175,000
1,375,000 . . .	1,750,000	175,000 . . .	200,000
1,750,000 . . .	2,125,000	200,000 . . .	225,000
2,125,000 . . .	2,500,000	225,000 . . .	250,000
2,500,000 . . .	3,325,000	250,000 . . .	300,000
3,325,000 . . .	4,175,000	300,000 . . .	350,000
4,175,000 . . .	5,000,000	350,000 . . .	400,000
5,000,000 . . .	6,075,000	400,000 . . .	450,000
6,075,000 . . .	7,150,000	450,000 . . .	500,000
7,150,000 . . .	9,275,000	500,000 . . .	600,000
9,275,000 . . .	11,425,000	600,000 . . .	700,000
11,425,000 . . .	15,000,000	700,000 . . .	800,000
15,000,000 . . .	20,000,000	800,000 . . .	900,000
20,000,000 . . .	25,000,000	900,000 . .	1,000,000
25,000,000 . . .	50,000,000	1,000,000 . .	1,250,000
50,000,000 . . .	87,500,000	1,250,000 . .	1,500,000
87,500,000 . . .	125,000,000	1,500,000 . .	1,750,000
125,000,000 . . .	187,500,000	1,750,000 . .	2,000,000
187,500,000 . . .	250,000,000	2,000,000 . .	2,250,000
250,000,000 . . .	333,325,000	2,250,000 . .	2,500,000
333,325,000 . . .	500,000,000	2,500,000 . .	3,000,000
500,000,000 . . .	750,000,000	3,000,000 . .	3,500,000
750,000,000 . .	1,000,000,000	3,500,000 . .	4,000,000
1,000,000,000 . .	1,250,000,000	4,000,000 . .	4,500,000
1,250,000,000 . .	1,500,000,000	4,500,000 . .	5,000,000

While the contents of a shortage report will depend largely on the nature of the loss and the methods utilized by the embezzler in defrauding his employer and concealing his crime, the following features must be adequately covered in each case:

1. Statement of the purpose of the examination of the records.
2. How, when, and by whom the defalcation was discovered.
3. The methods employed by the embezzler in defrauding his employer and concealing the crime.
4. A concise description of the various dishonest transactions, dates and amounts of the losses, any credits to be applied against such losses (salary due, commissions, bonuses, etc.), with supporting statements and exhibits.

The report should be so prepared that it may be readily understood by the average layman. Technical terms should be avoided in describing the routines and records; if such terms *must* be used, they should be adequately defined.

If there is a difference in the records that cannot be explained, there should be no hesitation on the part of those preparing the report about making a statement to this effect. A review of many shortage reports indicates that attempts are often made to augment the amount of the claim with large, unsupported differences and losses that could not, under any circumstances, be considered as coming within the terms of the bond. The purpose may be to overwhelm the bonding company; such practices are a waste of time and reflect unfavorably on the legitimate items in the claim.

Lester A. Pratt

The late Mr. Pratt was a nationally known specialist in employee fraud investigations. A certified public accountant for many years, Mr. Pratt's uncanny instinct for detecting the presence of fraud and trapping its perpetrators was made use of by many business-men, bankers, bonding companies and government supervisory agencies.

Mr. Pratt wrote and lectured extensively on many phases of accounting. His book, Bank Frauds—Their Detection and Prevention, *is regarded as the definitive work in that field. He also co-authored with Dr. George H. Newlove, of the University of Texas, a two-volume work,* Specialized Accounting.

Chapter 25

CCTV: CREATING A CLIMATE
FOR HONESTY

I.

How would you solve the problem of extraordinary temptation if you had—

- a shipping dock where loose, small boxes of valuable items were being loaded continually,
- mail to be opened that was filled with cash,
- returned goods areas where no inventory control of the merchandise was possible,
- sorting belts where small valuable items had to be handled rapidly on their way to shipping—again without the possibility of physical controls?

No matter how loyal or how honest the employee in such situations, the time could come when the urge to solve a family gift problem might be overpowering, and "just one item" would be put into a pocket. And for those with a true vocation for theft, the

---

© 1971, 1975, Security World Publishing Co., Inc.

opportunities in these situations would be almost limitless.

Aldens, Chicago, Illinois, one of the largest mail order houses in the United States, has all of these problems. They approached them with security measures that, starting in 1970, included the use of CCTV, and their results have been excellent.

CCTV can be used as a means of solving individual crime, and as an instrument of apprehension. There is also another aspect. While apprehensions were important in the Aldens installation, it was also clear that the great reduction in losses depended in large measure on the *deterrent effects* of the CCTV installations.

The first Aldens installation came after two years of persuasion to management that CCTV might be a good thing to try. The emplacement was made in the primary sortation area, where loose merchandise of all sizes and dollar values was exposed to pilferage. Very shortly after this installation, Aldens management asked their security officer, Dick Ostrowski, for his recommendation about further installations. Three more followed in short order. Management began to regard CCTV as a serious security tool, and the experiment stage was passed.

Special Problems Solved

Security in the various Aldens installations in Chicago was complicated by the seasonal nature of the employment curve. The number of employees varied from 2,500 to 5,000 in the course of a year. Allowing for the usual turnover, the base number of 2,500 employees could be considered permanent—the others were hired in response to seasonal peaks of demand. Rarely did the seasonal employee repeat. Most of the temporary group were new each year, and they presented increased security problems to the company, from within their own group and because of the effect they had on older employees. Thefts invariably increased considerably when large numbers of new help were taken on.

However, despite frustratingly vulnerable areas within the company and a large population of seasonal, transient employees, Aldens was still able to realize a substantial savings in losses in the four areas where CCTV was installed. For example, in 1969 one area had experienced a loss of X thousands of dollars. In 1970 the same area continued to experience losses, and by March that area already showed an amount equal to 18% of the total 1969 loss. In

March, 1970, the CCTV was installed. Total loss for the remainder of that year, March to December, amounted to 6% of the 1969 full year's losses. In 1971, the same unit showed a slight overage of $650, according to security personnel.

Vulnerable Area Covered

The Aldens experience includes four different warehousing situations in two different warehousing facilities. No retail areas were covered.

The first CCTV installation was tried at the primary sortation belt operation. At this location, the fourth installation was later made, in the women's lingerie section. Aldens's second installation was at the truck loading and shipping area, where a camera was set up in a shipping bay to look into trucks being loaded at the dock doors. The third CCTV installation was also at this location, in the receiving bay where returned goods were handled.

All merchandise moved out of the primary sortation operation sooner or later passes over the sortation belts. Employees in this area are therefore exposed to merchandise ranging from attractive small jewelry items to anything that might be covered in the 725 pages of the Aldens catalog—an inventory of two or three million items. It is the task of employees working these belts to put each item in a proper bin, so it can be carried by a tube system to other points of the company for shipping to the customer.

The primary sortation belt area is on the third floor of the building, in an elevated location. Two wooden stairways lead to a platform that contains two groups of four belts, with an aisle between each pair. Depending on the time of year, anywhere from four to fifteen people might be working on each side of the belt. The area is 100% concealed from open view, and anyone coming up for inspection could be detected by footsteps on the stairway.

Someone could always signal that somebody was coming, but if no supervisor was present, employees could take just about anything they wanted. Aldens reportedly considered it the most severe problem in that building.

Other security measures had been tried before the installation of CCTV. There was an exit check, and women employees were limited to small purses taken into the area. Yet much clothing disappeared from this area, as well as jewelry. The assumption was that an old dress might be taken off and thrown away, and a new one put on by the woman while she was working in the area. Small jewelry items might be easily hidden about the person in case a purse was inspected. Parabolic mirrors had been installed in an effort to survey the employees, but the problem remained. The employees could see the supervisor or security man watching them at the same time they were being watched in the parabolic mirrors.

In the primary sortation area, security applications experts recommended the installation of four cameras. Because of the floor plan, they were able to achieve 100% coverage of the belts with this number of CCTV cameras. Only one non-work area off to the side was left uncovered in the original plan. The deterrent effect was counted upon to make installation in that section unnecessary, but if the problem did not reduce immediately, a fifth camera could always be added in the last area.

The theft problem virtually disappeared immediately after installation. This overall effectiveness could be determined very rapidly, because thefts were first recognized by the receipt of empty packages in the areas for which they were sorted. Reports of empty boxes arriving in areas serviced by the primary sortation belt fell off immediately, and overall inventory figures confirmed the improvement later.

Another Kind of Installation

Security experts had hypothesized that in a warehousing operation with multiple rows or aisles there was little that could be done to prevent theft. In light of this opinion, the success of the Aldens installation over the 21 aisles in the women's lingerie area was impressive.

For example, in 1969 the area showed one of the highest losses in the company. In 1970, the dollar figures on loss continued to grow. After CCTV was installed, total losses for the remaining nine months of 1970 amounted to only a fractional percentage of the full year's losses for 1969.

In general, the security staff at Aldens feels that CCTV coverage is not effective unless it is 100%. The reason for this was that accomplished or determined thieves would soon learn the pattern of the camera and be able to steal in areas, or at moments, when the camera could not observe them. But this attitude presumed that the employee was able to determine where the camera was, and when it was watching. If the employee could not make this determination, he became uncertain about when stealing was "safe" and the temptation to steal was reduced.

In planning the installation in the women's lingerie area, great use was made of this deterrent effect. Twenty-one housings were installed, with all the necessary electrical connections and outlets for live use. Each housing was identical, made of plywood with a small glass window. One housing was installed at the end of each aisle. Cameras could be shifted about, and camera capability made it possible to cover any of the aisles—especially to watch specific problem areas.

The women's lingerie area apparently had only a few places where the problem was greatest, so 100% coverage was easily possible. Security officers had previously found that the sections holding women's bras in an average size, pantyhose, girdles, and other high-demand items suffered the greatest loss.

As the figures indicate, theft has been virtually eliminated in that area. Certain persons suspected of being involved in serious theft from confidential information received, left their jobs at Aldens after the installation of CCTV. One long-term employee who was known to have very expensive tastes moved out of an expensive apartment and sold his car after the CCTV was put in.

Several people were apprehended as the result of television monitoring, and some without, but all apprehensions were attributed to the CCTV monitoring, because that technique interrupted the "buddy system" of warning and interfered with various other internal arrangements that had made theft easier for the employees. The CCTV clearly created an enormous problem for the thieves in the area covered. To begin with, it forced them to get material out of the camera-covered area in order to steal it with a sense of safety. As the theft required more moves to be completed, it became easier to apprehend the culprits.

Since the initial apprehensions and the established success of the program in this 21-aisle area, problems have, in fact, been limited to a few small cases of employees who were "trying on" merchandise.

Returned Goods Area

CCTV cameras in the returned goods area are all pan, tilt and zoom. This area has approximately 20,000 square feet, with very high ceilings. The cameras must be able to cover from 50 to 100 employees, but at a cost that is still feasible. While the pan-tilt cameras offered substantial advantages in this situation, security application experts felt that those who were determined to steal would be able to tell when cameras were watching them and eventually pinpoint the split-second of time between camera cycles. Thieves could then slip away their merchandise at that point.

After brainstorming, the deterrent effect again emerged as the root of the solution. It was decided that if the employees could not see which way the camera was pointing, they would feel themselves in constant jeopardy and therefore be afraid to steal. Instead of a return to a system like the 21 housings found desirable in their women's lingerie area, it was decided to accept recommendations to put a glass or plastic mirror or bubble around the camera to conceal the direction that the lens was pointing.

On specifications from the security applications experts, Cadillac Plastics, Chicago, Illinois, eventually fabricated a 32-inch diameter plastic bubble of Plexiglas, smoke-grey in color. The bubble functioned something like sunglasses do in concealing the eyeball; it was impossible to determine the direction the camera was pointing, even when standing directly under the bubble that contained the camera.

The second day the system was operative, two apprehensions were made in a period of about 15 minutes. One employee had been with Aldens "for quite a while," and the company estimated that apprehension alone paid for the system—which had cost about $5,000 installed, for that area.

Dick Ostrowski points out that a camera whose pointing direction is unknown to the employees is "as good as having 500 cameras around." He adds by way of explanation, "Our business is so fast moving. You don't have dollar amounts identified in this particular area, because these are returns from customers. This is another area where the employees can be exposed to any type of merchandise we handle, including our most valuable jewelry items. In this area we can't determine whether we're losing anything or not, except by a customer's complaint. The customer would have to write to us and say, 'I sent in a so-and-so, and never received credit for it.' We can also judge something by the number of empty boxes we find in the bottom of mail bags or trucks, or other containers. But there is no direct inventory check at all.

"Since our CCTV installation, both the number of customer complaints and the number of empty boxes has diminished an appreciable amount."

Other Controls Also Used

Security on returned goods includes many measures in addition to CCTV. Because jewelry is the smallest and most valuable item, it is easiest to steal, and presents the greatest problem in losses. Once the packages are opened in the returned goods department and the jewelry is identified, it is restricted in its flow. Identified jewelry is taken from this returned goods department and hand-carried to a wired cage, where it is itemized and sent back to the appropriate department for return to inventory. Many jewelry items carried are in the $30 to $50 category, and the more expensive watches are as high as $125. In addition, Aldens carries movie cameras which are small enough and expensive enough to be an attractive item to thieves.

As a matter of general warehouse control, anything over $14.95 is handled in a restricted area where the order is filled, the billing made out, the packing completed, and the item put into locked cages and hand-delivered to the post offices in the Aldens building. Items over $14.95 per unit are shipped insured through the postal system. Anything under that price follows the regular system. However, items of lesser cost per unit are sent to the post office on a regular schedule so it is possible to keep track of them if necessary.

Truck-Loading and Shipping Docks

Two sides of the Aldens shipping location on West Roosevelt Road are covered by CCTV on the outside of the building. At these areas trucks are loaded with small parcels that are loose. Here, theft is identified only when the truck reaches its destination and the unloading operation discovers that many of the boxes are empty of merchandise.

In this area, the security experts did not recommend the use of a CCTV camera, but Aldens management insisted on it. Results were considered good when Chicago received a telephone call from an Aldens manager in Detroit, who said that his dock hadn't reported an empty box in three weeks—and he wanted to know what the Chicago end was doing to control the theft.

From that time until the closing down of the Detroit operation there were no reported shortages on shipments coming from the "D" dock in Chicago, loading for Detroit. Empty boxes were not found around the dock at either end, and no empty boxes were found in a washroom across from the dock, where the garbage cans used to contain many of them.

While the security people at Aldens had established light sources that beamed into the truck, there is some question about whether the picture itself was able to be totally effective in showing thefts. If nothing else prevented a clear view, the stacks of merchandise in the truck being loaded or unloaded provided an opportunity to hide theft. Again, the deterrent effect seems to have been a major factor in accomplishing such a high rate of loss reduction with the use of CCTV on this shipping dock.

That camera and one more were moved to another location where merchandise was again missing. The two cameras in this case were mounted in such a way that they could see very well into two trucks. Very little monitoring was done in this situation, be-cause of time. But again, the theft problem that had been very severe was eliminated.

Glen Collins, head of security at the sortation belt location, believes that the prime use of CCTV is as a deterrent. "But," he adds, "once in a while you have to refortify the deterrent effect by making an apprehension. And when the theft rate goes up, the security people do monitor more heavily and discover culprits."

II.

As part of their planning, the Aldens security staff had looked at all aspects of their CCTV installation, and they had come up with a few expectations. The first thing they waited for was overt reac-tion from employees. Surprisingly, they got none.

Despite an active and operative union, no official comments were made about the CCTV installations. Neither were any sizable indi-vidual reactions recorded. That the employees *knew* the equipment was there was established by what Dick Ostrowski refers to as the "normal reaction of people—who come up, look at the thing, make a couple of faces, and turn away. We also heard a couple of rumors like 'Who do they think I am?' or 'I've got enough people watching me now, let alone whatever that is.' " But these reactions seemed to be without rancor or hostility.

Apparently the cameras did tickle an occasional employee vanity, however. In one instance, a girl employed in an area for over two years who had never taken an extra job ticket, suddenly changed her attitudes. She had always completed her job tickets in plenty of time to handle more, but had preferred to idle away the extra time despite an increase in pay rate if she went over her quota. Shortly after the cameras were installed, however, this employee went to her supervisor and asked how she could get extra job tickets.

Second on the list of expectations of the Aldens security force was that no theft whatsoever would occur for a short time after the installation. Theft was expected to pick up again later on. But experience seemed to indicate that this expectation worked in reverse. Theft evidently continued on a sharply decreasing scale immediately after the CCTV installation, and then seemed to drop off virtually to nothing in surveyed areas.

However, the pattern did not apply identically to each of the four CCTV installations. Since the CCTV installations themselves were not identical, different amounts of time were required for employees to evaluate their chances for successful theft against each set of CCTV emplacements. The deterrent effect became stronger as the employees became more familiar with what the cameras could do. Finally, after initial apprehensions occurred, employee awareness of the function and possibilities of the installation increased rapidly, and the deterrent effect began to reach peak results.

Some Interesting Apprehensions

Actually, the first two apprehensions resulting from the initial installation were made close to 15 minutes after the system was working. One of these was an employee who had been with the company for quite a while. He was found with over $100 in watches in his pocket. The company reportedly considered that his apprehension in the returned goods area had paid for the entire system in that unit, which cost about $5,000.

In one case, the Aldens security force found that all thieves do not like to operate without attention—though presumably that attention would not go far enough to reveal the thief's identity. In one instance, Aldens had a problem with weird notes left on executive desks, personal property missing from the desks, and plants and other objects ripped to shreds on the tops of desks. The notes were signed "The Green Phantom." By carefully checking handwriting, security personnel narrowed their suspects down to one. But they still had to demonstrate that unacceptable acts were performed by the same person who left the notes. The notes alone were not a criminal offense.

The suspect was a member of the janitorial staff, so management was able to assign him special duties in the returned goods department, where the pan-tilt CCTV system was installed. That area would seem quite secure from observation, because it was surrounded by high walls and had all doors closed. He was entirely alone in the area, with ten or fifteen desks to be cleaned.

During the period of surveillance, security people very briefly turned away from the monitor, and the suspect disappeared from view. He had located the key to the jewelry cage in the drawer of one of the desks during that brief lapse in monitoring, and was now inside the cage stuffing items into his pockets. When he came out of the jewelry cage he spotted the camera. He walked over to it and made a disrespectful gesture just before he was apprehended. The suspect was a young man of 18 or 20 years who, when asked why he had left the weird notes and done the things he had, replied only that he had seen something like it on television.

In another case, a once-in-a-lifetime apprehension occurred because of an amusing bit of human curiosity, coupled with a video tape recorder attached to a CCTV camera.

As Glen Collins reports it, "We had a gentleman stealing watches, and you could see the details on the tape. But the security man watching the monitor, which was just about 200 feet from the site of the crime, had to leave his monitor to go and apprehend the gentleman who was stealing. He let the tape run. So the apprehension was witnessed, and the tape was still running during the time the security man was bringing the thief back for questioning.

"A day later, the security man decided to take a look at the apprehension on TV. He replayed the tape and saw one part that he didn't even know had been recorded. The fellow *next* to the thief he apprehended was on the screen while he had been walking back with the thief. The tape showed this other man standing there, looking around, and then running over to the side and taking watches out from under his pants and stuffing them underneath the table. So the security man knew that the other fellow was guilty, too, and he went out and apprehended him."

Planned Theft Controlled

While recognizing its successes, the Aldens security force still pointed out that only four areas in the company were covered with CCTV. If someone wanted to steal badly enough, there was always the possibility that he could move an object to some other part of the company and steal it from there. One of the prime security requirements for prevention of pilferage clearly was to prevent movement of employees within the company during working hours. Employees working in prime theft areas, particularly, would need to be restricted.

The Aldens experience demonstrates that theft is made considerably more difficult with the CCTV system. It becomes easier to discover and apprehend a thief, as well as to deter and provide a reduction in actual theft.

Further, when the video tape recorder is used in conjunction with the CCTV camera and the monitor, details are picked up that the watching officer may miss, or that he may not be at the monitor to see. This particularly applies to slipping of items from one employee to another, or the employee who leaves the area of camera surveillance with an item in his possession, to go to another area, where this item may be stolen. Such "pre-planning" is often limited by use of the CCTV camera.

While Aldens did not feel that they were beset by actual rings of thieves similar to groups discovered in some of the other major mail order houses, they did recognize that some of their employees were working together in internal "rings." Outside information had come to the security force reporting, "There's a store down the street selling an awful lot of Aldens merchandise." Often there was the additional comment that "so-and-so (an Aldens employee) had been hanging around there a lot." Several of the people so named were reported to have left their jobs after the CCTV was installed. For those who remained, the situation was obviously much more difficult for theft.

For the full 80 years of its lifetime, Aldens had had some kind of security. Actual records go back to about 30 years ago, showing that a more definitive security operation probably began at that time. However, until the last ten years or so, the company had a largely watchman type operation, with guards at entrances and exits, and guards patrolling to protect the premises from major invasions by burglars, fire, or other types of loss.

Today Aldens has a force of about 50 guards, which is broken down into stationary posts and patrols, and investigations. About eight or nine of the guards are on patrol and have the capability for investigation and apprehension. A battery of established security procedures exists and is followed today. It includes such things as truck sealing, personal identification, and exit checks of employees.

Observation Booths vs. CCTV

The general feeling in comparing the usefulness of observation booths with the CCTV installation seemed to be that CCTV must provide 100% observation. Because employees know the camera is watching them, if they are able to discover that the observation is not 100% they will figure out the pattern—and those who are theft-minded will be able to take advantage of it.

The mail order business is also subject to particular ills. One of the greatest of these stems from the mail sent in by the customers. Customers can not always pay by money order or check, or place their orders on credit, although the latter system is increasing. There are still many who send cash, and so the mail opening area presents serious problems of theft prevention, also.

Glen Collins describes security measures in the mail-opening section. "Our mail opening section has been covered with observation booths almost since its existence. We surveyed it for CCTV during the current group of installations, but we decided against it at present because the kind of work done there would require a very expensive installation—almost one camera per employee. And at times we have a couple of hundred employees up there."

Observation booths in this section contain carpets to avoid the obvious noise of patrolling monitors, and personnel have learned to be cautious of noise. Booths run across the ceiling, and permit the observer to watch the operators without interference. Hundreds of feet of mirrored observation fronts conceal the position of the security men patrolling the booths.

Collins feels that observation booths in the mail opening section seemed to have a deterrent effect similar to CCTV installation in other areas. Because a means was available for watching employees, and because employees could not determine whether the watching devices were being used, they were deterred from stealing. Again, it appeared possible to create a climate for honesty merely by the presence of surveillance devices that reminded the employees of the hazards and consequences of yeilding to temptation. Since the majority of employees were not seeking to steal as an end in itself, the over-all result was a substantial reduction in theft.

Additional Kinds of Security

An exit check is available in or out of any area where it is necessary. Employees are limited in the kinds and size of containers that they can carry into their work area, and the guard has the option of checking anything he finds questionable as it is being carried out. Small purses are specified for female employees, and if a purse looks unusually large or, presumably, if an employee is under suspicion, the guard has the option of checking that, also, as the employee leaves.

The Aldens employee identification program has been so successful that only on rare occasions has anyone been found present in a building who did not actually belong to the building.

Two identification cards are prepared for each employee. One is maintained in a file in the main lobby and the other is given to the employee as a pass. Since people can be forgetful, an employee may arrive at work stating that he forgot his pass, yet ask for admission. Because of the lobby identification card file, the guard on duty can immediately find the duplicate card, establish that the individual is indeed an employee, and safely admit him with a minimum of time lost.

Unexpected Side Effects of CCTV

Bemused security men had some difficulty maintaining physical possession of their CCTV installation at Aldens for a most unexpected reason. Management's skepticism took a sharp curve upward to total enthusiasm when they discovered it would be possible to catch jam-up areas on the production line through the television monitors. Monitors were moved from the security office to the production manager's office one floor above in very short order. Security personnel could, of course, continue to monitor from the production manager's office, or continue to make video tape recording whenever necessary.

All installations were not depleted by management enthusiasm. But a unique situation pertained with respect to the primary sortation belt. A 15-minute jam-up in that area could cause an 8-hour backlog for the entire company. Production management responded to the monitors with understandable eagerness because they saw an opportunity to forestall late deliveries caused by back-ups on the primary sortation belt. This could mean fewer orders lost through processing delay.

By turning on the monitor at periodic intervals, management was able to see the merchandise flow and anticipate a back-up. At first, the production manager telephoned a supervisor to add additional employees on the belts to help cover the load of excess merchandise. Later the system was simplified to paging, and all supervisors knew what to expect when they heard that page.

Glen Collins describes another unexpected side effect of the installation. "It was sort of like the child at Christmas who wants a bike—but somehow he gets a motorcycle. In the women's lingerie division the people are on an efficiency basis, so their efficiency directly relates to their salary, based on units per hour. Perhaps they hoped that they could compensate for some of the money they had been making by theft from that area, by increasing the earned money they made per week on salary. In any case, the operations manager from the women's lingerie section found that not only was theft decreased, but the production of his order fillers increased from 155 units per hour to 198 units per hour."

A third side-effect in saving and profit for the company was in the merchandise recount area. A continuous merchandise count is maintained for re-buying purposes. Personnel assigned to maintain inventory by re-buying are supplied with a count whenever the merchandise gets below a certain point. But when the difference between the book count and the physical count varies to any large degree, the order is sent back by the re-buyer for a recount. The manager of that department estimated that the savings in recount alone ran between $8,000 and $10,000 for the year 1970.

A fourth area of savings was realized in the prevention of back orders. For example, if an order is sent back for recount just because the re-buyer says "You say we're supposed to have 100, but we really only have 80," a great deal of re-checking on what happened to the 20 units of missing merchandise occurs. But if the record shows 80 units on hand, when the stock actually contained only 40 because of pilferage or other kinds of stock loss, that department will be unexpectedly out of a stock item, and a back order situation will be created. The curtailment in pilferage brought about by the CCTV security approach was reported to cut company back order expenditures in the area of several thousand dollars.

CCTV Cannot Replace Personnel

Security experts caution that the tendency for management to think that CCTV might also create a saving in the security budget by allowing a cut in people must be resisted by security directors themselves. They further point out that every effort should be made to avoid "selling" management on CCTV surveillance by suggesting that it would save personnel salaries. This type of installation must be thought of as a supplement that assists in the total security program, and not as a replacement for security personnel. First of all, there are always many areas where camera surveillance cannot be effective, and where security programs must be handled directly by people. Secondly, even in the areas covered by a CCTV installation, security people must be present to man the equipment. For proper monitoring and apprehension, security personnel are essential.

Overall Considerations

In any large operation, the number of problems multiplies because of the size of the floor space and the quantity of employees involved, to say nothing about variety and number of items in the inventory. But in a mail order operation, all of these factors are increased even more.

The security force for the company and security advisors such as the staff that arranged the installations at Aldens must keep many things in mind. They must learn to differentiate between a genuine security problem and other factors that might give the appearance of large scale thievery—such as mismanagement, poor inventory control, poor transport procedures, etc. In addition, they must consider personnel factors, and work for the protection of the employees while they do their job for the company.

There are two recurring reactions from almost every situation of employee theft. One is that the company made it so easy. The second is fear, when they realize the theft they considered so minor will cost them their job.

Given a deterrent effect that reduces the enormous temptation presented by valuable, often uncatalogued merchandise or cash available to the employee, and given the employee's genuine desire to keep his job and go on living normally, the company is apt to find, as Aldens did, that it is profitable to create a climate that encourages an employee to stay honest.

INDEX

Absenteeism, 39
Accounting practices, 235
Admissions, 157
   (See also Confessions; State-
    ments)
Age, as factor in internal theft, 87
Agency investigation
   background investigation, 106-
    108
   internal surveys, 106
   of internal theft, 106
   personnel research service, 110-
    111
   in pre-employment screening,
    210
   of problem employees, 106
   qualifications of investigators,
    107
   techniques, 108
   undercover, 93-94
Alcohol, 184-185
American Polygraph Association,
   172
Ash, Dr. Philip, 219
Audits, 55, 60, 78, 235-236

Background investigation
   (See Pre-employment screening)
Bank deposits, 234
Bankruptcy, 5
Birth certificates, 201

Cameras, motion picture, 108
   (See also Closed circuit televi-
    sion)
Cash handling, 232, 266
   and internal theft, 6
   petty cash fund, 236-237
   receipt control, 233-234, 243-
    244
Cash registers, 233
Citizenship papers, 201
Closed circuit television, 103,253-
   268
Collusion, 6, 60, 74, 106

Computer embezzlement, 7, 63-68
   safeguards against, 66-68, 245-
    248
   (See also Electronic data pro-
    cessing)

Confessions, 6, 115-116, 135-137
   defined, 157
   fear of confession, 137-139
   legal restrictions on, 150-156
   presence of counsel, 152-153
   reasons for, 144, 146-147
   and rules of evidence, 156-157
    (See also Admissions; State-
     ments)
Conflict of interest, 7
   (See also Executive dishonesty;
    Kickbacks)
Control methods, 9, 103
   audits, 76
   closed circuit television, 103,
    253-268
   for computer embezzlement, 66-
    68
   employee education, 12
   fidelity bonding, 76-77
   importance of, 93-94
   incentives, 11
   inventories, 76
   pre-employment screening, 76
   separation of responsibility, 76
   shopping services, 9
   undercover investigation, 9
   (See also Embezzlement controls)
Credit records, 200, 216
Criminal records, 200, 202-203,
   211-212, 216-217

Delivery controls, 241-242
Driver's license records, 203, 211
Drugs, 73, 186

Electronic data processing,
   245-248
    (See also Computer embez-
     zlement)

269

Other Security World Books of Interest . . . .

CONFIDENTIAL INFORMATION SOURCES: PUBLIC & PRIVATE
By John M. Carroll (352 pp.)

A unique, behind-the-scenes guide to the confidential personal information in public and private records. Reveals what information is on file, how it is gathered, who has access, how to identify the unknown persons. The security investigator's reference book.

INTRODUCTION TO SECURITY
By Gion Green and Raymond C. Farber (338 pp.)

A comprehensive introduction to the history, nature and scope of security in modern society. Details the basic principles of physical security, internal loss prevention, defensive systems, fire prevention and safety, with an overview of security services and the operations and career opportunities in specific areas.

SUCCESSFUL RETAIL SECURITY
An Anthology (303 pp.)

Employee theft, shoplifting, robbery, burglary, shortages, special fire problems, insurance recovery, and the nature of the retail security function — over 25 top security and insurance professionals pool their successful expertise in retail loss prevention, revealing exactly how loss occurs and how it can be prevented.

OFFICE & OFFICE BUILDING SECURITY
By Ed San Luis (295 pp.)

The first book of its kind devoted exclusively to the staggering security problems confronting today's offices, high-rise buildings and personnel. Analyzes external crimes and systems of defense, internal crime and protection against specific dangers, and the basics of modern office security.

ALARM SYSTEMS & THEFT PREVENTION
By Thad L. Weber (385 pp.)

First definitive treatment, in laymen's terms, of the so-called "impregnable" alarm systems, their strengths and weaknesses, how they are attacked by criminals, and the techniques required to defeat these attacks. A highly readable guide to the entire gamut of alarm problems.

HOSPITAL SECURITY
By Russell L. Colling (384 pp.)

Complete protection of people and property in health care facilities. Developing a practical, detailed program for establishing a security system or refining existing programs to deal with hospital vulnerabilities, including: theft of drugs, assault, kidnaping, fire, disaster, strikes, robbery, accidents, vandalism, internal theft, more.

HOTEL & MOTEL SECURITY MANAGEMENT
By Walter J. Buzby II and David Paine (256 pp.)

Security hazards in the hotel industry, and protective measures which can help the hotel or motel, large or small, prevent losses. Includes theft, holdup, fraud, fire, disaster, restaurant and bar security, access control. Special emphasis on laws affecting hotels, including innkeeper's liability for injury to guests due to accident or crime.

In addition to its hard cover books on security subjects, Security World Publishing Company publishes *Security World* and *Security Distributing & Marketing (SDM)* magazines; produces booklets, manuals and audio tape cassettes on security; and sponsors the International Security Conference, held annually in Chicago, New York and Los Angeles. Books and other materials are available from Security World Publishing Co., Inc., 2639 So. La Cienega Blvd., Los Angeles, California 90034.